Early English Women Writers 1660–1800

Early English Women Writers 1660–1800

Agnes Beaumont, *The Narrative of the Persecutions of Agnes Beaumont*
(ed. by Vera J. Camden)

Cornelia Knight, *Dinarbas*
(ed. by Ann Messenger)

Priscilla Wakefield, *Mental Improvement*
(ed. by Ann B. Shteir)

Eliza Haywood, *Three Novellas*
(ed. by Earla A. Wilputte)

Frances Burney, *The Witlings*
(ed. by Clayton J. Delery)

FRANCES BURNEY

THE WITLINGS

Edited with Introduction and Notes
by Clayton J. Delery

COLLEAGUES PRESS
EAST LANSING

Early English Women Writers 1660–1800: No. 3

ISBN 0-937191-55-8
Library of Congress Catalog Number 93-79538
British Library Cataloguing-in-Publication data available
Copyright 1995 by Clayton J. Delery
All rights reserved

Published by Colleagues Press Inc.
Post Office Box 4007
East Lansing, Michigan 48826

Distributed outside North America by
Boydell and Brewer Ltd.
Post Office Box 9
Woodbridge, Suffolk IP12 3DF
England

Printed in the United States of America

CONTENTS

PREFACE

Frances Burney, who was famous during her life because of her novels, and who has been famous since that time because of her diaries, letters and journals, has never been famous for her plays. Yet she left behind a total of seven, consisting of comedies (*The Witlings*; *A Busy Day*; *Love and Fashion*; and *The Woman Hater*) and tragedies (*Edwy and Elgiva*; *Hubert de Vere*; and *The Siege of Pevensey*). Another tragedy, *Elberta*, exists only in a preliminary form.

None of these plays was published during Burney's lifetime, and only one, *Edwy and Elgiva*, was ever produced. That play, a tragedy, had a tragic reception; when it was performed in 1795 it ran for one night only and was "hooted off the stage" (Thrale, *Thraliana* 2: 916). An edition of *Edwy and Elgiva* was prepared by Miriam J. Benkovitz, and published by The Shoe String Press in 1957. In the same year, the plot of *Elberta* was reconstructed by Marjorie Lee Morrison in a doctoral dissertation at the University of Texas. The comedies, however, continued to be ignored, in spite of the periodic attention of a number of scholars, most of whom felt that the comedies were far superior to the tragedies. As early as 1950, Joyce Hemlow, who would later write the indispensable biography, *The History of Fanny Burney*, published an article dealing with the importance of the Burney plays ("Fanny Burney: Playwright"). In *Fanny Burney*, Michael Adelstein devotes a great deal of attention to the Burney comedies. Hemlow and Adelstein believe Burney's *A Busy Day* to be the best of the comedies, and Tara Ghoshal Wallace's edition of this play was published by Rutgers University Press in 1984. However, other Burney comedies, most notably, *The Witlings*, have excited interest. In *Literary Women* Ellen Moers writes of the day she embarrassed herself by laughing out loud while studying in the Berg Collection as she read *The Witlings*. She believes the play demonstrates that Burney's true gift may have been for the drama, not the novel, and on the basis of this play, Moers allows herself the luxury of speculating what might have happened to English drama if Jane Austen had followed Burney's lead in the theatre instead of the novel (117–118). In *Feminism in Eighteenth-Century England*, Katharine Rogers discusses

vii

The Witlings and goes so far as to call the play "Burney's best sustained imaginative work" (26).

The current edition of *The Witlings* has been prepared in the belief that this is the most interesting—and the best—of the Burney plays. It was Burney's first creative project following the publication of *Evelina*, and it thus forms a largely unknown bridge between *Evelina* and Burney's next novel, *Cecilia*. In fact, the name Cecilia was taken from the heroine of *The Witlings* after it was apparent that the play would never be performed.

The Witlings was also written as a direct result of the members of the Streatham group urging Burney to try her hand at the stage. When the manuscript of the play began to be circulated, their shock at the sharpness of the satire did not obliterate their pleasure in its quality. It was, to use the words of Adelstein, "exactly the play that the Streathamites knew that she could write, urged her to write, and hoped she would write" (59). Both Richard Brinsley Sheridan and Arthur Murphy actively solicited the play for production, and the interest of two such prominent theatre men is, by itself, a testament to their perception of Burney's dramatic talent.

Perhaps more important to current scholarship, particularly on women writers, is the fact that the play is largely a satire on the Bluestockings. Katharine Rogers has noted a certain perversity in the impulse that led a literary woman to make fun of literary women (*Feminism* 47). The sharpness of the satire, particularly the acerbic portrait of Lady Smatter (who resembles Mrs. Elizabeth Montagu, the "Queen of the Blues") is, at least in part, what eventually led Burney's Father, Dr. Charles Burney, and his friend, Samuel Crisp, to forbid production of the play. This gives *The Witlings* importance as a document which questions literary values of the time, and which raises interesting questions about female authorship. In a century which was notable both for satire and for a rise in female literary activity, why was *The Witlings* considered a shockingly inappropriate play for a young woman to write? The answer apparently lies in the play itself, which thus becomes a reflection of Burney's perceptions of her own authorship, and of the position of literary women in the eighteenth century.

ACKNOWLEDGMENTS

I cannot list or express my appreciation to all of the people who have had a hand in this project, but certain persons have made outstanding contributions toward seeing that I complete this work.

First, I would like to thank the faculty members of the Graduate Center of the City University of New York who comprised my dissertation committee. My advisor, Professor David C. Greetham, spent many hours reading and evaluating various states of my editorial and critical work, and Professors Robert Day and Rachel Brownstein contributed many interesting and insightful comments and ideas. I must also gratefully acknowledge Professor Lars Troide of McGill University for his many contributions to this project in his editorial, critical and advisory capacities. Thanks also go to Martin Stevens, Gerhard Joseph, Speed Hill, Richard McCoy, Morris Dickstein and Lynn Kadison. I could not have completed this work without the the assistance and cooperation of the late Dr. Lola Szladits, curator of the Berg Collection of the New York Public Library, and her successor, Francis O. Mattson. Finally, I would like to give thanks to my parents for their support and encouragement through the twenty-three years of my formal education, and to Charles Triche and Lucette Holland for seeing to it that I had a comfortable, companionable, and peaceful working environment while I completed this project.

INTRODUCTION

FRANCES BURNEY: PLAYWRIGHT

> Mrs. Thrale then returned to her charge, and again urged me about
> a comedy; and again I tried to silence her, and we had a fine fight to-
> gether; till she called upon Dr. Johnson to back her.
>   "Why, madam," said he, laughing, "she *is* writing one. What a rout
> is here, indeed! she is writing one upstairs all the time. Who ever
> knew when she began *Evelina*? She is working at some Drama, de-
> pend upon it."
>   "True, true, O king!" thought I. (*Diary and Letters* 1: 90)

The Burney family was very fond of the theatre and the performing arts, and there was much in the life of the young Burney children
to enhance and develop their interest in the drama. Frances's father,
Dr. Charles Burney, was a musician, and although his own pursuits
were largely scholarly rather than performance-oriented, Dr. Burney
composed, in 1750 and 1751, the music for a variety of after-pieces
and masques, largely at the request of his good friend, David Garrick.
Dr. Burney's theatre career was cut short when illness forced the
family to move to King's Lynn, but it resumed in the 1760s when
they returned to London, until Charles Burney finally decided to stop
writing music for the stage in 1767 (Stone and Kahrl, 378-379).
Thereafter he limited his career to teaching music and to writing
scholarly books about the history of music.

Because he was recognized as both a fine teacher and a fine
scholar, Dr. Burney had contact with people of wealth, fame, and influence in London society, and many of those people were guests in
the Burney home. The guests who attended one of Dr. Burney's mu-
sical evenings might have included Dr. Johnson, Hester and Henry
Thrale, Garrick, the great vocalists Agujari and Gabrielli, and the Ital-
ian music teacher, Signor Piozzi; in fact, we know from Frances Burney's *Early Diary* and her *Memoirs of Dr. Burney* that the Burney
family introduced Piozzi to Hester Thrale, thereby unintentionally ini-
tiating one of the most famous love affairs of the eighteenth century
(*Early Diary* 2: 284-287 and *Memoirs* 2: 101-114).

One of the more frequent—and most loved—visitors to the Burney home was the famous actor-manager, David Garrick. He was known to all the Burney children from their youth, and their mutual fondness and regard did not end as the children grew older. Frances recorded the following scene in January, 1772, at which time she was nineteen years old.

> Mr. Garrick is this moment gone. Unfortunately my Father was out, & Mama not come down stairs—Yet, to my great satisfaction, he came in.— Dick ran to him as the Door was opened—we were all seated at Breakfast.— 'What! my Bright Eyed Beauty!' cried he—& then flinging himself back in a Theatric posture—'& here ye all are—one—two—three—four— Beauties all—' He then came in, & with a great deal of humour, played with Dick—How many pities that he has no Children, for he is extremely, nay passionately fond of them. (*Early Journals and Letters* 1: 183-4; see also *Early Diary* 1: 150)

All the Burney children seem to have attended the theatre from a very early age, which, as Joyce Hemlow notes in *The History of Fanny Burney*, was anywhere "from the age of three or four" (12). They were fortunate that their father's warm relationship with Garrick led to their being given frequent invitations to sit in the Garricks' private box. There the children saw Garrick perform in many roles. Garrick also performed some of these roles in the Burney home, where he sometimes gave the children instruction in the art of mimicry. Joyce Hemlow writes that "Before they could read they acted over parts they had seen him play; when they could read, they got parts with the utmost facility for their private theatricals. . . . Their interest in drama and the standards of acting that they formed from Garrick's performances lasted their lives long" (*History* 13).

Frances Burney was regarded by the family as the best of the mimics, although her gift was one that very few outside of the family circle would ever see. With other people, Frances was shy to almost total silence, and her manner was markedly composed and grave. In fact, by the time she was eleven, her silence and gravity had earned her the nickname "The Old Lady" (*Memoirs* 2: 168), and by her fifteenth year a Mr. Seton of their acquaintance nicknamed Frances "the silent, observant Miss Fanny" (*Early Diary* 1: 39 n.; *Early Journals and Letters* 1: xvi; *Diary and Letters* 6: 400; *Journals and Letters* 11: 286).

Her powers of observation were probably cultivated at least partially through necessity; Frances received almost no formal education, and although it has been recorded that at age eight she did not yet know her letters, she was able to memorize speeches and passages of poetry just from hearing her brothers and sisters repeat them (*Diary and Letters* 6: 400). Indeed, mimicry and memorization were the two areas in which she excelled in her childhood. By the age of ten, she had not only learned her letters, but had begun "scribbling incessantly, little works of invention; but always in private" (*Memoirs* 2: 123). This secret activity went unremarked by her parents, and later in life her father would describe her as being "wholly unnoticed in the nursery for any talents or quickness of study" (*Memoirs* 2: 168).

Frances began composing stories, poems, and speeches in her head even before she could read and write. As soon as she learned how, she began committing them to paper. All Burney scholars know the story of how at the age of fifteen Frances was forced by her stepmother (who disapproved of young girls spending time at writing) to stop her scribbling. At that time, Frances burned her juvenile novel, *The History of Carolyn Evelyn* (the story of which provides the background for *Evelina*). She also burned, in her own words, "Elegies, Odes, Plays, Songs, Stories, Farces,—nay Tragedies and Epic Poems" (*Memoirs* 2: 124).

Some nine months after the flames of the bonfire had died, Frances was beginning to scribble again; her first project was a diary, which she addressed to "Nobody," writing, in part:

> to Nobody can I reveal every thought, every wish of my Heart
> . . . . No secret *can* I conceal from No—body, & to No—body can I be
> *ever* unreserved. . . .The love, the esteem I entertain for Nobody, No-
> body's self has the power to destroy. From Nobody I have nothing to
> fear, the secrets sacred to friendship, Nobody will not reveal, when
> the affair is doubtful, Nobody will not look towards the side least
> favourable. (*Early Journals and Letters* 1: 2; see also *Early Diary*
> 1: 5-6)

The chosen form of address, aside from being humorous and spirited, is simultaneously self-deprecating, self-effacing, and suggests a sense of isolation relieved through writing. It also provides a useful strategy for dealing with the meddlesome Mrs. Burney; one can imagine her asking Frances, "To whom are you writing?" and Frances primly responding, "Nobody."

Burney's early writings are of interest for many reasons, not the least of which is their display of Frances's powers of observation, memory, and mimicry, and the ways in which she was able to employ those gifts in a dramatic, or quasi-dramatic, format. Although she records her participation in conversations when necessary, she often minimizes her participation or does not participate at all. The "silent, observant Miss Fanny" was able to turn her shyness to good use, for her quiet demeanor frequently allowed her to be more observer than participant, and let her use her abilities in memory and mimicry to record speech patterns, idiosyncratic characterizations, and entire conversations, first in her mind, and later in her diary.

Her familiarity with stage conventions even included some amateur experience as an actress in family theatricals. For example, one description of such a production occupies fifteen pages in the *Early Journals and Letters* (2: 235-253; see also 2: 262-263 and *Early Diary* 2: 164-179). The modern-day reader, however, should not be misled by the term "amateur," for it was an ambitious production, and the performers took their roles very seriously; the evening began with an overture by a band, the mainpiece that evening was Arthur Murphy's *The Way to Keep Him*, and the afterpiece was Henry Fielding's *Tom Thumb*.

Frances's knowledge of the London stage and of dramatic conventions undoubtedly made her realize how important dialogue and dramatic setting could be to her writing; indeed, two unpublished doctoral dissertations explore the connections between Burney's non-dramatic works and the drama of the time. In *Fanny Burney and the Theatre* (1957), Marjorie Lee Morrison discusses Burney's familiarity with theatre and her use of dramatic techniques in diaries, letters, novels, and plays, and Elizabeth Y. Mulliken's *The Influence of the Drama on Fanny Burney's Novels* (1969) finds that Burney was "best as a novelist when she was most fully a dramatist" (191-192).

Burney's use of dramatic techniques was not accidental; in *The History of Fanny Burney*, Joyce Hemlow presents draft versions of several scenes of *Evelina*, and then contrasts them with published versions of the same scenes, as a means of illustrating the ways in which Burney achieved characterization through refining and rethinking dialogue and speech patterns, and through the writing "voice" of Evelina herself, which could almost be said to be a series of soliloquies, and through which almost all information in the novel is presented to the reader (79-85). Thus, as Hemlow notes:

> Evelina speaks no more of *Horse-Laughs*, therefore, but of *loud laughter*; refers not to the *parlour* but to the *drawing room*; not to *every fright* in it but to *whoever was old or ugly*; not of *home strokes* but of

sarcasms. She decided to say that Lord Orville made choice of her rather than that he fixed upon her. . . . There is a difference between the Evelina who said 'I was so mad at this sneering speech that I had hardly patience to make any reply,' and the one who wrote more carefully 'I was so much disconcerted at this sneering speech that I said not a word.' (84)

The fact that the novel is epistolary, and is, in fact, dominated by the letters of Evelina, prohibits any analysis of actions or motives through an omniscient narrator. Evelina must interpret her world and transmit her interpretation to the reader according to what its inhabitants do and, perhaps more importantly, according to what they say and how they say it; it is for this reason that Burney was necessarily so concerned with the way the characters spoke. Hemlow writes:

> undignified expletives like 'Faith' are removed from Lord Orville's utterances. . . . Sir Clement Willoughby's speeches are also repaired, relieved of abruptness, and augmented as he assumes importance as the villain of the piece. . . . The conversation of the fop, Mr. Lovel, already close to the language of the stage, is further rounded out with catchwords, mild oaths, and ejaculations. Such revisions helped to individualize character. (82–83)

The care that Burney took to individualize character through diction resulted in the vivid portraiture of even minor characters, and it was this vividness that caused so many of the early readers of *Evelina* to be struck by the "life and manners" contained in the book. The ability to characterize through speech and dialogue first caused Mrs. Thrale to suggest to Burney that she write a play, and that made Dr. Johnson laughingly speculate that she had already begun to write one (*Diary and Letters* 1: 90). Dr. Johnson's remark was made in jest, but there was more truth in that jest than he could possibly have known.

Just as Burney's writing had anticipated Johnson's jest, she also anticipated him in the subject matter; a short time later, Burney wrote

> he enjoyed [his thought] inwardly, without heeding our curiousity, — till at last he said that he had been struck with a notion that "Miss Burney would begin her dramatic career by writing a piece called 'Streatham.'"
>
> He paused, and laughed yet more cordially, and then suddenly commanded a pomposity to his countenance and his voice and added, "Yes! 'Streatham—a Farce!'" (*Diary and Letters* 1: 101–102; see also volume 3, *Early Journals and Letters*, forthcoming)

Other Streathamites were interested in seeing Burney try to write
a play; in fact, the first time that Hester Thrale brought Frances together with Richard Brinsley Sheridan he urged her to try her hand at
comedy:

> Mr. Sheridan.—What then are you about now?
> F[rances] B[urney].—Why, twirling my fan, I think!
> Mr. Sheridan.— No, no; but what are you about at home? However,
> it is not a fair question, so I won't press it.
> Yet he looked very inquisitive; but I was glad to get off without any
> downright answer.
> Sir Joshua [Reynolds].—Anything in the dialogue way, I think, she
> must succeed in; and I am sure invention will not be wanting.
> Mr. Sheridan.—No, indeed; I think, and say, she should write a
> comedy.

A little later Burney writes:

> F.B.—Oh!—if you both run on in this manner, I shall—-
> I was going to say get under the chair, but Mr. Sheridan, interrupt-
> ing me with a laugh, said,
> "Set about one? very well, that's right!"
> "Ay," cried Sir Joshua, "That's very right. And you (to Mr. Sheridan)
> would take anything of hers, would you not?—unsight, unseen?"
> What a point - blank question! who but Sir Joshua would have ven-
> tured it!
> "Yes," answered Mr. Sheridan, with quickness, "and make her a
> bow and my best thanks into the bargain." (*Diary and Letters* 1:
> 194-195)

It was quite a testament to the raw dramatic talent that Sheridan
perceived that he was willing to say, even in jest, that he would take
a comedy from her "unsight, unseen." On another evening shortly
following, Arthur Murphy seconded Sheridan's opinion:

> "If I," said Mr. Murphy, looking very archly, "had written a certain
> book—a book I won't name, but a book I have lately read—[*Evelina*] I
> would next write a comedy."
> "Good," cried Mrs. Thrale, colouring with pleasure; "do you think
> so too?" (*Diary and Letters* 1: 203-204)

Although Burney's comedy was apparently already underway, the
encouragement from such figures as Sheridan and Murphy was undoubtedly both reassuring and, to Burney, a little frightening; as she
wrote upon yet another occasion of being urged to try comedy,

"after so much honour, so much success—how shall I bear a downfall?" (*Diary and Letters* 1: 126-127).

She would soon have to learn, for although she would complete her play, it was never to be performed. Burney's comedy is similar to the farce proposed by Dr. Johnson in that it concerns the foibles of a group of writers and scholars who have formed a literary coterie and named it The Esprit Party. This group was apparently not intended to resemble specific people who frequented Mrs. Thrale's salon at Streatham, but early readers of the play perceived resemblances to other London wits of the time. These resemblances ultimately kept Burney's first comedy, *The Witlings*, from finding its way to the stage.

Whether or not *The Witlings* would have succeeded must forever remain a matter of conjecture, but it is possible to examine the play in terms of the popular forms of comedy at the time, which might suggest its potential stageworthiness. Among new mainpieces being staged at this period in the history of the London theatre, the comedies tended to fall into one of two broad categories, those being Laughing Comedies and the Sentimental or "Weeping" Comedies, the latter of which were sometimes referred to as *Comédies Larmoyantes*.

Ernest Bernbaum traces the Sentimental Comedy[1] back to the first performance at Drury Lane of Colley Cibber's *Love's Last Shift*, at which an audience that expected to laugh at the follies of mankind found instead that they were brought to tears by the story of a long-suffering wife, Amanda, and her reconciliation with her profligate husband, Loveless. In *The Drama of Sensibility*, Bernbaum notes that "the play was an astonishing novelty, not merely because it was a comedy at which they wept, but because it aroused admiration for people like themselves. It exhibited faith in the natural impulses of contemporary middle-class audiences" (2). This play demonstrates many of the traits associated with Sentimentalism: belief in the basic virtue and perfectibility of mankind; moral didacticism; a sense of pity for the suffering; and suitable rewards for the virtuous (Bernbaum 2-10). Bernbaum's assertion that Sentimental Comedy was, for

---

[1]Sentimentalism would also affect tragedy, with some representative plays being *Jane Shore* and *The London Merchant, or, The History of George Barnwell*.

a time, the reigning mode in mainpieces has been challenged in *The Rakish Stage*, written by Robert D. Hume, who attacks this assertion by examining a key document that has been traditionally used to uphold it: Oliver Goldsmith's "An Essay on the Theatre: or, A Comparison Between Laughing and Sentimental Comedy." Goldsmith was certainly no stranger to Sentimentalism, as he demonstrated in his poem, "The Deserted Village." But two years after writing "The Deserted Village," Goldsmith would describe Sentimental Comedies as being those

> in which the virtues of Private Life are exhibited, rather than the vices exposed; and the Distresses rather than the Faults of Mankind make our interest in the piece. . . . If [the principal characters] happen to have Faults or Foibles, the Spectator is taught, not only to pardon but to applaud them, in consideration of the goodness of their hearts; so that Folly, instead of being ridiculed, is commended, and the Comedy aims at touching our Passions without the power of being truly pathetic. (*Collected Works* 3: 212)

Hume, arguing that the "Comparison" is a triumph of style over substance, suggests that Goldsmith was voicing objections to a largely imaginary dominance of the Sentimental mode, and that Bernbaum was responding to Goldsmith's rhetoric rather than to the plays themselves, most of which are not Sentimental Comedies (312–358).

The other major comic genre was Laughing Comedy in which, to employ Goldsmith's terminology, the vices of private life are exhibited, rather than the virtues exposed, and the faults rather than the distresses of mankind make our interest in the piece. While Hume suggests that the perceived dichotomy between the two genres has some use, he cautions that classification of individual works is difficult, and sometimes impossible, as satiric "Laughing" comedies might have sentimental elements, and many "Sentimental" comedies include broadly funny scenes (Hume 332–333, 339). The difference, as Hume sees it, is not so much a difference in subject matter as in the way it is handled (321). Laughing Comedies might be safely said to include such works as Goldsmith's own *She Stoops to Conquer*, Sheridan's *The School for Scandal*, and Hannah Cowley's *The Belle's Stratagem*. In these plays all the suitable lovers are eventually allied, but the audience views the final scenes through tears of laughter rather than tears of pity or joy. It is to this tradition that *The Witlings* belongs.

The play, like other Laughing Comedies, does have some sentimental elements. In a letter written shortly after the completion of the play, Burney's sister, Susan, reported the family's reactions to it— how "Charlotte laugh'd till she was almost black in the face, at Codger's part," and how, to Susan's mind, "the Serious part seem'd even to improve upon me by [the second hearing], and made me for to cry in 2 or 3 places—I wish there was more of this Sort—so does my Father—so I believe does Mr. Crisp" (quoted in Doody, *Frances Burney: The Life in the Works*, 92; also in Hill, *The House in St. Martin's Street*, 150-151). But in spite of the scenes which brought the family to tears, the play seems markedly more satiric than sentimental in tone.

Some scholars who have worked with the play, such as Elizabeth Yost Mulliken and Marjorie Lee Morrison, have expressed doubt as to whether or not *The Witlings* would have succeeded on the stage, but it seems apparent that their pessimism is based in part upon a misreading of the genre. For example, Mulliken discusses a scene in which "While Mrs. Voluble and her friend Mrs. Wheedle and Bobby enjoy a hearty meal, Cecilia, in visible contrast to their brutish lack of sensibility, is quite unable to eat because she is upset" (36) Mulliken's use of the term "sensibility" betrays a desire to read Cecilia as a Sentimental Heroine, yet there are indications that Cecilia's "sensibility" is being ridiculed. Such parody of literary form was not unknown to Burney; in the *Early Journals and Letters*, for example, we find at least one extended example of her parody of the "sublime" style (1: 4; see also xviii,n.). In her edition of Burney's *A Busy Day*, Tara Ghoshal Wallace illustrates the ways in which Burney makes fun of that play's heroine, Eliza, and "her desire to be an unexceptionable sentimental heroine" (5; see also 6-8). As for *The Witlings* itself, consider the following passage, in which a milliner approaches the recently bankrupt Cecilia about an unpaid bill:

> *Mrs. Wheedle.* Won't you please, ma'am, to look at the Bill?
> *Cecilia.* Why should I look at it?— I cannot pay it,— I am a destitute Creature,— without Friend or resource!
> *Mrs. Wheedle.* But, ma'am, I only mean—
> *Cecilia.* No matter what you mean!— all application to *me* is fruitless,— I possess nothing— The Beggar who sues to you for a Penny is not more powerless & wretched,— a tortured & insulted Heart is all that I can call my own!

Mrs. Wheedle. But sure, ma'am, when there comes to be a Division among your Creditors, your Debts won't amount to more than—
Cecilia. Forbear, forbear!— I am not yet inured to Disgrace, & this manner of stating my affairs is insupportable. *Your* Debt, assure yourself, is secure, for sooner will I famish with want, or perish with Cold,— faint with the fatigue of labor, or consume with unassisted Sickness, than appropriate to my own use the smallest part of my shattered Fortune, till your— & every other claim upon it is answered.
Mrs. Wheedle. Well, ma'am, that's as much as one can expect (5.1. 159-177).

Mrs. Wheedle's request for payment may be a bit tactless, and possibly even a bit "brutish," but given an earlier discussion of Mrs. Wheedle's difficulties in getting customers to pay their bills, her actions here are certainly understandable. Further, Cecilia's overly-dramatic speeches are nicely contrasted with Mrs. Wheedle's dry response. In such passages, it is difficult to believe that Cecilia is not being satirized.

Majorie Lee Morrison, like Mulliken, believes the portrayal of the lovers is sentimental (92-93). But in a Sentimental Comedy, the resolution would, almost by definition, have to be achieved through the recognition of their inherent worth by the antagonist, Lady Smatter. In fact, Lady Smatter never experiences such a recognition, and her eventual consent to the union of Beaufort and Cecilia is the result of social blackmail and intellectual bribery.

Probably the best published discussion of the play occurs in Margaret Doody's biography, *Frances Burney: The Life in the Works.* Doody calls the play "intelligent" and "brilliantly devised," and suggests that it anticipates the theatre of the absurd (90-91). She also, not incidentally, believes that the play is strong enough to be successfully staged today.

Ultimately, the readers of *The Witlings* will have to make their own judgments. But whether potentially stageworthy or not, whether it is a Sentimental Comedy or a Laughing Comedy, it is clear that the publication of *The Witlings* is long overdue.

THE SUPPRESSION OF THE WITLINGS

"Oh, Dr. Johnson!" cried I; "'tis not for nothing you are feared."

"Oh, you're a rogue!" cried he, laughing, "and they would fear *you* if they knew you!"

"That they would," said Mrs. Thrale; "but she's so shy they don't suspect her. . . . But I have been telling her she must write a comedy; I am sure nobody could do it better. Is it not true, Dr. Johnson?" (*Diary and Letters* 1: 89)

Why, then, was *The Witlings* never produced? The play was not merely forgotten, but was intentionally suppressed, due primarily to the efforts of Frances's father, Dr. Charles Burney, and his friend, Samuel Crisp, to whom Frances affectionately referred as her "Second Daddy." There have now been several theories advanced in an attempt to explain their desire to see the piece suppressed, all of which have some degree of surface validity, but none of which, by themselves, appear to tell the whole story.

For many years the suppression of the piece was explained by means of a bit of direct commentary in the Burney Diaries—commentary to the effect that the play was thought by Samuel Crisp to resemble Moliere's *Les Femmes Savantes*, while not being as good. Burney's play and Moliere's play both derive humor from the exploits of learned women, but this is a fact of which Burney pleaded ignorance, for she claimed that, before writing *The Witlings*, she had neither read nor seen *Les Femmes Savantes* (*Diary and Letters* 1: 259 n.). In any case, the resemblance between the plays does not go far beyond this rather surface feature, for the plots of the two are markedly different. Moreover, as Margaret Doody has noted, the humorous portrayal of studious women had been successfully employed by other English dramatists, including William Congreve (in *The Double Dealer*), John Gay and Alexander Pope (in *Three Hours After Marriage*), and Susannah Centlivre (in *The Basset Table*), among others (Doody 81).

Crisp's remark that *The Witlings* resembled *Les Femmes Savantes* does not seem to appear in any letters or documents; in fact, the story may be something of a red herring, designed to lead people away from the truth. Burney scribbled this explanation for suppression in the margin of her personal papers some years after the play was written. It is possible that Crisp actually said or wrote something to this effect, but other evidence suggests that Crisp and Dr. Burney had less impersonal reasons for seeing to it that the piece was never performed.

One theory, originally advanced by Thomas Babington Macaulay in his essay, "Madame D'Arblay," is that Samuel Crisp argued the case for suppression because he himself had not been a successful drama-tist, and was thus jealous of Frances Burney (or anyone else) attempt-ing to succeed where he had not. This theory rests on the erroneous premise that Crisp spent the entire latter part of his life in bitter seclusion due to the failure of his tragedy, *Virginia*. Joyce Hemlow tells us, however, that his retirement was actually due to financial rather than artistic concerns (*History* 17). Moreover, although Crisp was not happy with the reception of his play, Annie Raine Ellis noted in her edition of Burney's *Early Diary* that Crisp's tragedy was not, by the standards of the day, a dismal failure at all. It was not only per-formed eleven times in its first season at Drury Lane (a quite re-spectable record in itself), but was subsequently revived at both Drury Lane and Covent Garden, and it was printed three times within Crisp's lifetime (*Early Diary* 1: xli–xliii, and 2: 325–332).

Other possible explanations for Dr. Burney's and Mr. Crisp's de-sire to suppress the play are almost certainly connected with per-ceived resemblances some of the characters in *The Witlings* bore to people actually living, and this may be deduced from a letter Samuel Crisp wrote to Frances Burney in which he recommended that she not waste any time in trying to revise the piece; instead, he suggested another project for her, which was a comic novel based on the hu-morous misadventures of a family known to the Burney household. Crisp pressed his case with the words:

> there [seem] to me an inexhaustible fund of matter for you to work on, and the follies of the folks [are] of so general a nature as to furnish you with a profusion of what you want to make out a most spirited, witty, moral, useful comedy, without descending to the invidious and cruel practice of pointing out individual characters and holding them up to public ridicule. (*Diary and Letters* 1: 263)

The most recent suggestions concerning the identities of these "individual characters" were advanced by Margaret Doody in her bi-ography, *Frances Burney: The Life in the Works*. Doody believes that Dr. Burney may have been uncomfortably aware of similarities between Lady Smatter, one of the major characters of the play, and his own wife, who was Frances Burney's stepmother, and of whom

Frances does not appear to have been fond. Doody has suggested that Lady Smatter and Mrs. Burney resemble each other in that both women were overly fond of society and had a tendency to make themselves conspicuous in company (*Frances Burney: The Life in the Works* 96-97). Doody also traces some resemblance between a character by the name of Dabler and Frances's father. Dabler is a hack poet, possessed of little or no talent, who courts favor from influential women by shamelessly flattering them in less-than-inspired verse. In fact, his only talents are for rendering himself obsequious and for touching on the vanities of the women whose patronage he desires. Dr. Charles Burney differs from Dabler in that he was a fine musician, an enormously talented teacher and scholar, and an extremely hard-working man. However, he depended on the patronage of the wealthy and influential for his living; they were the people who provided him with pupils and they were the people who bought his books. Like Dabler, he sometimes courted the favor of prominent women by composing verses in their honor, and also like Dabler, he was sometimes perceived as obsequious (Doody 97-98).

If Dr. Burney did see something of himself and his wife in *The Witlings*, and if this was his motivation for wishing to suppress the piece, it was not something that he acknowledged or brought to his daughter's attention. Instead, another resemblance was found which was sufficiently disturbing to warrant a degree of concern and which preyed upon Frances's fears of being ridiculed for her literary efforts, but one which was far enough removed from family matters so that it could be used as an argument for suppression without troubling domestic relations. Dr. Burney and Mr. Crisp apparently seized upon the character of Lady Smatter, but rather than compare her to Dr. Burney's wife, they compared her to another lady, the well-known Bluestocking, Mrs. Elizabeth Montagu. The similarities between Lady Smatter and Mrs. Montagu are sometimes quite striking—even more striking than the resemblances between Smatter and Mrs. Burney; the latter, although an undeniable social and familial presence, does not seem to have been noted either for literary attainments or for pretensions to such. Lady Smatter, on the other hand, centers her whole life on literary study, and this overriding trait or "humour" determines everything she does in the course of the play. It is also one of the things Lady Smatter has in common with Mrs. Montagu, and it is because of this similarity that Dr. Burney's and Crisp's comparison of Lady Smatter and Mrs. Montagu was so weighted.

In fact, of *The Witlings*, Hester Thrale once wrote "I like [the play] very well for my own part, though *none* of the scribbling Ladies have a Right to admire its general Tendency" (*Thraliana* 1: 381 emphasis added). The plot of the play is a variation on the portionless heroine theme—a theme that was very popular for late eighteenth-century fiction. In *The Witlings*, Cecilia Stanley, a wealthy and well-bred young woman, is engaged to be married to a young gentleman named Beaufort. Beaufort is the nephew and adopted son of Lady Smatter. In the second act of the play, Cecilia learns that her fortune has been lost due to the bankruptcy of her guardian, Stipend. Beaufort wishes to proceed with the union, but Lady Smatter forbids marriage to Cecilia, saying to him, "Never suppose I adopted you to marry you to a beggar" (2.1. 652-653). The rest of the play is concerned largely with Cecilia's efforts to avoid social and personal disgrace, Beaufort's efforts to locate and marry Cecilia, and Lady Smatter's efforts to keep Beaufort and Cecilia apart.

Lady Smatter, besides being Cupid's nemesis, is also a chief member of a literary coterie called The Esprit Party, and it is the portrayal of Smatter and her party to which Thrale alluded in her remark about the "Scribbling Ladies." Lady Smatter's literary group resembles several that were functioning at the time that Burney wrote *The Witlings*, the two most famous of which were Hester Thrale's literary salon based in her home at Streatham, and another, larger group which met in various homes in and around London and which was known as the Blue Stocking Society. Neither group was a "club" in the accepted sense of the word, for neither had any charter or official membership, and many people were known to be connected with both groups. These groups were noted for consisting of men and women who would assemble and associate rather freely within the drawing room instead of following the then-current custom of grouping all the women at one end and all the men at the other. Conversation, particularly literary conversation, was the aim of such meetings, and those two all-pervasive entertainments of eighteenth-century society—gambling and politics—were outlawed (Busse 49-50). People who might be found at these gatherings included Dr. Johnson, Boswell, Frances Burney and her father, Dr. Charles Burney, Sir Joshua Reynolds, Hester Thrale, Hester Chapone, Hannah More (who would immortalize the group in her poem, *The Bas Bleus*), Elizabeth Carter, Edmund Burke, Horace Walpole, any number of actors, writers and musicians, as well as assorted *beaux esprits* of both sexes.

Elizabeth Robinson Montagu was a prominent member of the Blue Stocking Society. In fact, so great was her notoriety that she would eventually earn the title, "The Queen of the Blues."[2] As the fictional Lady Smatter and the historical Elizabeth Montagu were both prominent women notable for engaging in literary pursuits, it would be natural to find points of resemblance between them, although such a comparison would be by no means either inevitable or exclusive of other women. In fact, when Hester Thrale read the play she said "I believe this rogue means me for Lady Smatter" (Burney, *Diary and Letters* 1: 219). Yet there were indications that Lady Smatter resembled Elizabeth Montagu more closely than she did any other literary woman of that time.

Lady Smatter devotes her life to the Esprit Party and to the study and criticism of such authors as Pope and Shakespeare. Within the play, however, the extent of Smatter's learning is mocked, as she constantly mangles or misattributes quotations from Shakespeare, Pope, Swift, or other authors whose work she claims to know. Elizabeth Montagu, like Lady Smatter, was wealthy, influential, and an indefatigable participant in literary society. Although she was undeniably well-read and intelligent, Montagu seems to have made her greatest contributions by creating an atmosphere in which wits could associate genially, and by providing pecuniary assistance to improvident writers. She was a tireless hostess, ready to entertain two *beaux esprits* or several hundred at a given time. And Montagu and such of her associates as Mrs. Vesey, Mrs. Carter, and Mrs. Boscawen were largely responsible for creating a social environment in which literary women could associate freely, and in some degree of equality, with literary men. This had the effect of sanctioning female learning and female authorship in a way that it had never been sanctioned before.

But just as Lady Smatter is portrayed as a poor master of her craft, Mrs. Montagu's own attempts at authorship and criticism were not al-

[2]The title "Queen of the Blues" was not intended to be a compliment, for it was bestowed sarcastically as a result of a literary feud between Dr. Johnson and Mrs. Montagu. Since that time, Montagu's supporters and detractors have both used the title, each adapting it for their own purposes. No matter how Montagu's "coronation" initially came to pass, the fact that Johnson could so name her, even in derision, marks her prominence in the literary world. For an account of the feud, see Burney's *Diary and Letters* 1: 498–502 and 2: 236.

ways enthusiastically received. Her work did not go unnoticed or un-
praised, but some of the compliments she received were noticeably
tepid, if not double-edged. When Lord Bath had finished reading
Montagu's dialogue, "Bernice and Cleopatra," and was returning the
then unpublished manuscript, he wrote: "I would sooner have answer'd your letter and sent you back the enclosed Dialogue, but that
I went out to take the air in my chaize. You may depend upon my se-
crecy, but should it ever be published, it will be known to be yours,
because nobody else can write like it" (Montagu, *Letters*,
[1720-1761] 1: 237).

In 1769, Elizabeth Montagu published what would be her most famous work, *Essay on the Writings and Genius of Shakespear*. Although *The Critical Review* wrote that Montagu was "almost the
only critic who has yet appeared worthy of Shakespeare" (cited in
Scott 66), other people held opinions that were not quite so enthusi-
astic. When Sir Joshua Reynolds commented to Dr. Johnson that the
Essay did Mrs. Montagu honor, Dr. Johnson replied, "Yes Sir; it does
her honour, but it would do nobody else honour" (Boswell, *Life of
Johnson* 2: 88). On another occasion Johnson commented that Montagu's *Essay* was so bad that neither he nor Mrs. Thrale could complete it, a remark that caused a great deal of embarrassment to Thrale
(then Hester Piozzi) when Boswell published it in the *Life of Johnson* (5: 245).

It eventually became fashionable to ridicule Montagu, and she was
portrayed in contemporary satires as being a person of mean intellectual accomplishments. When Cumberland characterized the intellec-
tually inept "Vanessa" in his *Observer*, nearly everyone of importance
in London recognized Montagu as Vanessa's original. Burney, then
serving at the court of Queen Charlotte, provided a rather qualified
defense for Montagu with the words, "Whatever may be Mrs. Montagu's foibles, she is free, I believe, from all vice, and as a member of
society she is magnificently useful" (*Diary and Letters* 3: 71). Montagu eventually became so closely, and unfairly, identified with shallow learning that one writer has stated that Montagu's "sham attainments brought ridicule on all [the Blue Stockings]" (Lobban 462),
and it has sometimes been suggested that she is almost solely responsible for the term "bluestocking" having become one of derision.

But the factors in the Smatter characterization that point most def-
initely to Montagu have to do with matters other than literary. In *The
Witlings* Lady Smatter is childless and has adopted her nephew,

Beaufort, as her son. Beaufort will inherit the Smatter fortune upon Lady Smatter's death, provided that he behaves as she wishes in the meantime. Like Lady Smatter, Elizabeth Robinson Montagu was a widow possessed of a vast fortune. Because her only child had died many years earlier at the age of fifteen months, Mrs. Montagu had adopted her nephew, Matthew Robinson. He was made an heir on the condition that he assume the name Montagu, so that it might be perpetuated[3] (Montagu, *Letters* [1762-1800] 1: 301).

When Burney had completed her play, having already shown all or part of it to various members of the Streatham set, she sent it to the two critics whose approval she most desired and whose judgment she most feared: Dr. Charles Burney and Samuel Crisp. She entrusted the manuscript to them with the words "I should like to have three lines, telling me, as nearly as you can trust my candour, its general effect. After that, take it to your own desk, and lash it at your leisure" (*Diary and Letters* 1: 256).

Dr. Burney and Mr. Crisp seem originally to have enjoyed the play, and a letter from Susan Burney to Frances describes a scene which occurred when Dr. Burney read the manuscript to the family—twice. Although the family preferred the first three acts to acts four and five, the consensus was that the characters were well-drawn and that much of the dialogue was quite witty (see Hill, *The House in St. Martin's Street* 150-151; see also Doody, *Frances Burney* 92).

After the reading, Dr. Burney and Mr. Crisp discussed the play privately. Exactly what they said may never be known, but they apparently lashed a bit more than anticipated, for Frances's next letter to Dr. Burney begins "'down among the dead men' sink the poor *Witlings* for ever and for ever and for ever!" (*Diary and Letters* 1: 256). She goes on to write: "I expected many objections to be raised—a thousand errors to be pointed out—and a million of alterations to be proposed; but the suppression of the piece were words I did not expect; indeed, after the warm approbation of Mrs. Thrale

---

[3]In Burney's second novel, *Cecilia*, the heroine inherits a fortune from her uncle, but a clause in his will stipulates that she can retain the money and property only if any man she marries agrees to assume *her* family name. The realism of this clause has sometimes been questioned, but the case of Matthew Montagu, born Robinson, illustrates that such things did sometimes occur.

and the repeated commendations and flattery of Mr. Murphy, how could I?" (*Diary and Letters* 1: 256–257)

The full content of Dr. Burney's comments on the play is unknown, but in an unpublished letter, Dr. Burney says that his "chief and almost only quarrel [is with] The Blue Stocking Club Party [and] not only the whole piece, but the plot had best be kept secret"[4] (quoted in Hemlow, *History* 137, and in Doody, *Frances Burney* 95). Doody believes that Dr. Burney may have disguised his true feelings and motives for arguing suppression, and she suggests that Dr. Burney's professed fear of the Bluestockings' reactions amounted to a form of emotional blackmail, through which he implied that Frances would be hurting him as much as (or more than) herself in producing the play (*Frances Burney* 97). Frances Burney's response was:

> I really think, even more than myself, the astonishing success of
> [*Evelina*] would, I believe, even more than myself, be hurt at the failure
> of [*The Witlings*]; and I am sure I speak from the bottom of a very honest heart when I most solemnly declare that, upon your account any disgrace would mortify and afflict me more than upon my own; for whatever appears with your knowledge, will be naturally supposed to have met with your approbation, and, perhaps, with your assistance; therefore, though all particular censure would fall where it ought—upon me—yet any general censure of the whole, and the plan, would cruelly, but certainly, involve you in its severity, (*Diary and Letters* 1: 257)

For a while it seemed as though *The Witlings* would not die; both Murphy and Sheridan continued to voice their interest in the manuscript, and Dr. Burney began to consider allowing Frances to produce a revised version of the play (an act which may contradict Doody's ar-

---

[4]When Burney noted that Mr. Crisp discouraged production because of a resemblance between her play and *Les Femmes Savantes* (see *Diary and Letters* 1, 259 n.), it is possible that she was still, many years later, trying to obey her father's injunction and diverting attention away from Montagu and the Blues by supplying another "cause" for suppression. If this is the case, it is interesting that she may have supplied a clue to future readers of the *Diary* by naming another play concerning the exploits of learned women. It is also interesting that she did not destroy the manuscript of the play or the letters concerning it, as she did, for example, with the potentially sensitive papers concerning the Thrale-Piozzi marriage, or the ones which reveal her own distaste for the second Mrs. Burney.

gument that the play made him personally uncomfortable). It was at this point that Frances submitted to Mr. Crisp a list of planned revisions for the play. Among those changes, she was planning:

> To entirely omit all mention of the club;—
> To curtail the parts of Smatter and Dabbler as much as possible;—
> To restore to Censor his £5000[5] and not trouble him to even offer it;—
> To give a new friend to Cecilia, by whom her affairs shall be retrieved, and through whose means the catastrophe shall be brought to be happy;—
> And to change the nature of Beaufort's connections with Lady Smatter, in order to obviate the *unlucky* resemblance[6] the adopted nephew bears to [Mrs. Montagu] our female pride of literature. (*Diary and Letters*, 1: 316 emphasis added)

Mr. Crisp, in marked contrast to Dr. Burney, was unfaltering in his determination that the piece be suppressed. In an effort to keep the play from the stage he wrote: "The omissions you propose are right, I think; but how the business of the piece is to go on with such omissions and alterations as you mention, it is impossible for me to know. What you mean to leave out—the club and the larger share of Smatter and Dabbler—seems to have been the main subject of the play" (*Diary and Letters*, 1: 322).

Because of Crisp's objections, *The Witlings* was abandoned. Burney began working on her second novel, *Cecilia: Or, Memoirs of an Heiress*. She took the first name of her heroine from the play, and the plot lines of novel and play both concern young women whose lives and fortunes are controlled by absent or inadequate guardians. About 1801–1802, after Montagu's death, Burney tried to use the character of Lady Smatter in a comedy titled *The Woman Hater*. Lady Smatter

---

[5]Censor is the character whose actions resolve the conflict of the play, and one thing he does is to give Cecilia £5000 so that she will not remain completely portionless. Burney was aware of the implications of such a gift from a man to an unmarried woman; in fact, Censor and Cecilia have a very guarded conversation on just that subject. Although Censor denies any dark motive, and although the audience is supposed to believe in both Censor's honor and Cecilia's virtue, it was apparently thought that the incident still suggested immorality.

[6]Note, however, that Burney calls the resemblance "unlucky," rather than "unintentional."

emerges as a more sympathetic character in the later play, but that, too, was never performed or published.

Whatever Dr. Burney's and Mr. Crisp's private motives may have been, if they were ultimately able to convince Frances that production was unwise, it was because they were able to act on her fears concerning possible damage to her reputation and the possible repercussions she might have faced. What forms might these repercussions have taken?

If we assume that Mrs. Montagu had perceived Lady Smatter as a stage portrayal of herself, a production of *The Witlings* might have hurt Burney in four ways. The economics of stage production in this period were not greatly dissimilar to those of subscription publishing in that both depended directly upon public favor; the playwright generally received no money up front, but was instead paid out of the proceeds of the third, sixth, and ninth nights of production in the first season. If the Smatter and Esprit portrayals had been perceived as an attack, it is not inconceivable that Montagu and others may have abstained from attendance and persuaded their friends to abstain as well, thereby causing a financial loss to Burney. Moreover, if the play were read as an attack on noted literati, sales and reviews of Burney's next novel, *Cecilia*, would undoubtedly have suffered. In the 1790s, Burney would publish her third novel, *Camilla*, partially by subscription, knowing that a successful subscription would pay far more than an advance sale to a publisher. Among those who subscribed to *Camilla* were a number of noted Bluestockings, including Mrs. Montagu, who almost certainly would not have subscribed if they felt they had been insulted in *The Witlings*.

Finally, a production might have provoked an immediate reprisal in the form of a lampoon, the potentially humiliating effects of which are discussed, ironically enough, in the play itself. In fact, it is particularly ironic that Burney's awareness of the danger of literary pursuits forms a central theme of *The Witlings*.

DESCRIPTION OF MANUSCRIPT AND
METHODOLOGY EMPLOYED

Description of the Manuscript

The manuscript of *The Witlings*, written in Burney's own hand, is catalogued in the Berg Collection as follows: "Arblay, Frances Burney d'. The Witlings./ A comedy. Holograph, unsigned and undated." The manuscript consists of five folio notebooks of Burney's own fashioning, each one containing an entire act of the play. All of the notebooks consist of a single gathering, and because each one has exactly the number of leaves it needs to contain its act, the number of sheets of paper used to make them does not remain constant; the number ranges from 7 to 11 and one-half sheets, producing notebooks of 14 to 23 leaves.[7]

The notebooks have not been sewn together; a microfilm copy of the manuscript prepared by The Berg shows that the sheets of at least some of the notebooks were originally held together with a loosely tied cord. The cord is gone, and many of the leaves have torn apart at the original fold, but those leaves that are still intact remain loosely inserted within each other. The bottom right hand margin of each leaf contains the catchword as an aid to reading and collation.

All the notebooks are of slightly different dimensions, and the paper used to make them is of three different manufactures: Notebook I is made of paper bearing a watermark consisting of the initials

---

[7]Act III has an extra half-sheet insert which forms the second leaf of the notebook, and which contains part of the text. The notebook containing Act V was at one time covered with an extra half-sheet which was pasted to the rest and which bears the inscription N 23/The Witlings 1779/see Diary Vol. 1 page 242. This half-sheet is no longer attached to the rest of the manuscript, and may not have been an original part of the notebook. The first two lines of this inscription (N 23/The Witlings 1779) appear to be in Burney's hand, apparently as part of the systematic cataloguing of family papers undertaken at the end of her life. The third line (see Diary Vol. 1 page 242) is by a later hand, and refers to the *Diary and Letters*, as edited by Charlotte Barrett, which was published after Burney's death in 1842. Volume 1 page 242 contains letters and notes concerning the suppression of the play. The corresponding page in the 1904 edition of the *Diary and Letters* (the edition used here) is Volume 1, page 259.

"G.R." underneath a shield, with chain lines that are 2.6 cm. apart, running perpendicular to the fold; Notebook II is made of paper bearing the watermark "C. Taylor" and has chain lines 2.8 cm. apart, running perpendicular to the fold; Notebooks III-V are made of paper which contains a watermark consisting of the initials "T.C." with chain lines 2.7 inches apart, running perpendicular to the fold. All sheets in these notebooks are made of this paper, except the center sheet of Notebook IV, which bears the same watermark (the initials "G.R." beneath a shield) as Notebook I.

The collation formulae of the notebooks are:

> 14
> I. $2°$ 18.5 cm. × 23.4 cm. 1^r The/Witlings/A/Comedy./By/*A Sister of the Order*. 1^v, Dramatis Personae. 2^r-28^v, text of act I, pp. 1-26, catchwords.

> 16
> II. $2°$ 18.7 cm. × 23.5 cm. 1^r-32^v, text of act II, pp. 27-56, catchwords.

> 1 [+1] 3-17
> III. $2°$ 18 cm. × 22.4 cm. 1^r-34^v, text of act III, unpaginated [pp. 57-90], catchwords.

> 16
> IV. $2°$ 18.2 cm. × 22.9 cm. 1^r-32^v, text of act IV, unpaginated [pp. 91-122], catchwords.

> [1+] 2-23
> V. $2°$ 18.6 cm. × 22.5 cm. 1^r N23/The Witlings 1779/ see Diary Vol.1 page 242, 1^v blank, 2^r-23^r, text of act V, (23^v, blank), unpaginated [pp. 123-165], catchwords.

Methodology

If *The Witlings* had not been suppressed, its immediate fate would have been stage production, not publication. In an article titled "Playwrights' Intentions and the Editing of Plays," T.H. Howard-Hill argues that principles used in editing a production manuscript are not necessarily the same as those used in editing a manuscript intended for publication. He states that "Any script written before trial in the theatre is necessarily provisional and—in terms both of theatrical practicalities and authorial intention—more likely to be 'incorrect' in some degree than complete and correct" (269). Keeping this argument in mind, I have not attempted to edit the play as though Burney had prepared it for immediate publication; instead, I have treated the play as a "working copy," altering only those few errors and irregularities which might have impeded understanding of the text. These are the principles that I have followed:

At the point where each page of Burney's manuscript comes to an end, a bracketed notation within the reading text identifies the leaf and its recto or verso side (e.g. [3v] or [4r]). As Burney wrote each act of the play in its own notebook, the notation [3v] occuring in the text of the third act would indicate the end of the verso (back or reverse) side of the third leaf of Burney's notebook for Act III.

I have numbered the lines of the play in order to aid the reader in locating emendations and textual notes, all of which appear at the bottom of the page. Words or references that might be unfamiliar to the reader are glossed there whenever possible. The same is largely true of quotations and literary allusions; however, as the characters in the play are "witlings" rather than "wits," many of these quotations and allusions are incorrect, and in frequent instances I have been unable to discover a probable source. No attempt to "correct" infelicitous quotation and attribution has been made as such infelicities are important to both the characterizations and the theme of the play.[8]

There are a number of deletions and excisions in the manuscript. Some occur when Burney chose to substitute one word for another, or when she wished merely to eliminate a word or two from the sen-

---

[8] A detailed discussion of this editorial concern appears in G. Thomas Tanselle's "External Fact as an Editorial Problem" which appeared in *Studies in Bibliography* 32 (1979): 1–47.

tence. In these cases, Burney's corrected version is the one appearing in the reading text, and the original reading is provided in the notes.

However, Burney was planning revisions of the play after her father and Mr. Crisp originally forbade its production, and in the manuscript there are several longer passages that are marked for possible excision, and that tend to occur in places where the satire directed against Lady Smatter and the Esprit Party is particularly biting. Some of these excisions are indicated through a system of symbols that Joyce Hemlow encountered in editing the *Journals and Letters* (see Hemlow's essay, "Letters and Journals of Fanny Burney: Establishing the Text"; see also the introduction to Lars Troide's recent edition of *The Early Journals and Letters of Fanny Burney*), and other passages are included within sets of brackets, or have had lines pencilled through them. I have included all such passages within the reading text, indicating them through the use of pointed brackets.

The play contains a number of stage directions meant to indicate how a particular line of dialogue is to be read. Some of these precede the line of dialogue, as is the custom today, and others follow it, as in the following example:

> Censor. You have but little reason if you understood me.
> *aside.*

As an aid to the modern reader I have silently regularized these directions so that all precede the line of dialogue, and I have placed stage directions within parentheses. It was Burney's usual habit to indicate stage directions in italic (i.e. through underlining), with proper names and the word "Exit" indicated in bold italic. She was not always consistent in these practices, so I have silently regularized the use of bold italic, and where Burney neglected to italicize a stage direction, I have done so and have noted the emendation.

The manuscript contains the long "s" (which resembles the modern "f") whenever an "s" is doubled in a word. I have reduced the long "s" to the modern short version. I have silently emended the punctuation of the page containing the *Dramatis Personae*, and have headed the acts consistently with Roman numerals (rather than the mixture of Roman and Arabic numerals Burney used), as these features fall outside of the action and dialogue of the play. Several other features (the use of "&" for "and" or the use of a digit rather than the written name of a numeral) may seem eccentric to the modern reader. Tara Ghoshal Wallace silently emended these features in her edition of *A Busy Day*, on the grounds that an eighteenth-century compositor would have done the same (see Wallace 175–177). While this is true, these eccentricities would not have been perceived when spoken, nor do they pose difficulty to the reader. Since the manuscript's immediate destiny was to be stage production instead of publication, I have followed the manuscript forms.

I have followed Burney's punctuation, including her extensive use of the dash, and have emended it only in a very few cases where her punctuation seemed erroneous and might impede the understanding of modern readers. All such emendations have been recorded. Likewise, I have followed Burney's capitalization as closely as I was able, altering her form only in very rare cases (such as when a proper name does not have an initial capital letter), and then listing the emendation in the textual notes.

Textual emendations are located by line references at the bottom of the page on which they occur, and are illustrated through a lemma system. The reading to the left of the lemma (]) is the one in the edited text, and that to the right is the manuscript reading. Authorial revisions to the play can be discerned by the abbreviations *ins* (insertion), *del* (deletion), *cor* (correction), and *or* (original reading). For example, where Burney has substituted "up" for "out", the note reads "up] *ins*, out *del*". Editorial emendations are illustrated through the use of the abbreviations *MS* (manuscript), + (followed by), *lc* (lower case), and *cap* (capital). For example, a note reading "Know] *lc MS*" would indicate that a word appearing with an initial capital letter in the edited text was not capitalized in the manuscript; as another example, "provocation. Relieve] ~ , + *lc*." indicates that the period following "provocation" in the reading text replaces a comma in the manuscript (in order to correct a comma-splice), and that the word following this comma (Relieve) is not capitalized in the *MS*. See the list of abbreviations and symbols for further details.

The manuscript contains very few illegible words for which a reading must be conjectured, and very few places in which an additional stage direction has been placed as an aid to the reader. All such conjectures and additions are placed in square brackets.

ABBREVIATIONS AND SYMBOLS

cor	correction to the text
del	deletion from the text
ins	insertion
or	original reading that was subject of later correction
MS	reading as it appears in the manuscript
+	followed by
cap	a letter originally capitalized in MS
lc	a letter originally lower case in MS
~	edited text and manuscript in agreement
|	break in at the end of a line of manuscript
/	indicates the end of a manuscript page.
r	recto (front) side of a manuscript leaf
v	verso (reverse) side of a manuscript leaf
< >	material within is marked for excision in the manuscript.
[ ]	material within is a conjectural reading or an editorial insertion.

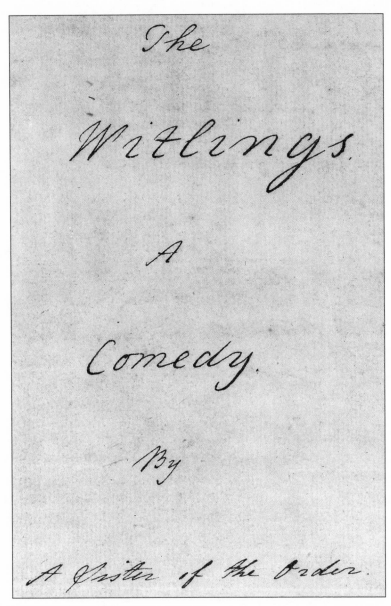

Title page of manuscript. Reproduced courtesy of the Henry W. and Alfred A. Berg Collection, The New York Public Library, Astor, Lenox and Tilden Foundations.

The

Witlings.

A

Comedy.

By

A Sister of the Order.

Dramatis Personæ .

Beaufort.
Censor.
Dabler.
Jack, half Brother to Beaufort.
Codger, Father to Jack, & Father in Law to Beaufort.
Bob, Son to Mrs. Voluble.
[Footmen, Servants, and Messengers]

Lady Smatter, Aunt to Beaufort.
Cecilia.
Mrs. Sapient.
Mrs. Voluble.
Mrs. Wheedle, a Milliner.
Miss Jenny, her aprentice.
Betty, Maid to Mrs. Voluble.
[Miss Sally.]
[Miss Polly.]
[A Young Woman.]

Act. I.

Scene, A Milliner's Shop.

A Counter is spread with Caps, Ribbons, Fans &
Band Boxes. **Miss Jenny** & several young
women at Work.
Enter ***Mrs. Wheedle****.*

Mrs. Wheedle. So, young ladies! pray what have you done to
Day? (*she examines their Work.*) Has any body been in yet?

Miss Jenny. No, ma'am, nobody to Signify;— only some people a foot.

Mrs. Wheedle. Why, Miss Sally, who is this Cap for?

Miss Sally. Lady Mary Megrim, ma'am.

Mrs. Wheedle. Lady Mary Megrim, Child? Lord, she'll no more
wear it than I shall! why how have you done the Lappets?
they'll never set while it's a Cap;— [2r] one would think
you had never worked in a Christian Land before. Pray, Miss   10
Jenny, set about a Cap for Lady Mary yourself.

Miss Jenny. Ma'am I can't; I'm working for Miss Stanley.

Mrs. Wheedle. O ay, for the Wedding.

Miss Sally. Am I to go on with this Cap, ma'am?

Mrs. Wheedle. Yes, to be sure, & let it be sent with the other
things to Mrs. Apeall in the Minories; it will do well enough
for the City.

Enter a ***Footman****.*

Footman. Is Lady Whirligig's Cloak ready?

Mrs. Wheedle. Not quite, Sir, but I'll send it in 5 minutes.

---

16 Minories: a street occupied in this period by a comparatively affluent
working class. See M. Dorothy George, *London Life in the Eighteenth Century* (New York: Harper & Row, 1964), 65-67, 318, 342, 412.

Footman. My Lady wants it immediately; it was bespoke a   20
     Week ago, & my lady says you promised to let her have it
     last Friday.

Mrs. Wheedle. Sir it's just done, & I'll take care to let her La-
     dyship have it directly.   ***Exit Footman.***

Miss Jenny. I don't think it's Cut out yet.

Mrs. Wheedle. I know it i'n't. Miss Sally, you shall set about it
     when you've done that Cap. Why Miss Polly, for goodness'
     sake what are you doing?

Miss Polly. Making a Tippet, ma'am, for Miss Lollop. [2v]

Mrs. Wheedle. Miss Lollop would as soon wear a Halter: 'twill   30
     be fit for nothing but the Window, & there the Miss Nota-
     bles who Work for themselves may look at it for a Pattern.
                    *Enter a **Young Woman**.*

Young Woman. If you please, ma'am, I should be glad to look
     at some Ribbons.

Mrs. Wheedle. We'll shew you some presently.
                    *Enter **Mrs. Voluble**.*

Mrs. Voluble. Mrs. Wheedle, how do do? I'm vastly glad to see
     you. I hope all the young Ladies are well. Miss Jenny, my
     dear, you look pale; I hope you a'n't in Love, Child? Miss
     Sally, your Servant. I saw your Uncle the other Day, & he's
     very well, & so are all the children; except, indeed, poor   40
     Tommy, & they're afraid he's going to have the Whooping
     Cough. I don't think I know that other young lady? O Lord
     yes, I do,— it's Miss Polly Dyson! I beg your pardon, my
     dear, but I declare I did not recollect you at first.

Mrs. Wheedle. Won't you take a Chair, Mrs. Voluble?

Mrs. Voluble. Why yes, thank you, ma'am; but there [3r] are
     so many pretty things to look at in your shop, that one does
     not know which way to turn oneself. I declare it's the great-
     est treat in the World to me to spend an Hour or two here
     in a morning; one sees so many fine things, & so many fine   50
     folks,— Lord, who are all these sweet things here for?

31-32 Miss Notables: *notable* was used to describe women who are "capable,
managing, bustling" (*Oxford English Dictionary*, hereafter *OED*). Compare
with the use, of "Mrs. Notable" in Burney's *A Busy Day* (I.282. p. 41 and n.).

Mrs. Wheedle. Miss Stanley, Ma'am, a young lady just going to
be married.

Mrs. Voluble. Miss Stanley? why I can tell you all about her.
Mr. Dabler, who Lives in my House, makes verses upon her.

Miss Jenny. Dear me! is that Gentleman who Dresses so smart
a Poet?

Mrs. Voluble. A Poet? yes, my dear, he's one of the first Wits
of the age. He can make verses as fast as I can talk.

Miss Jenny. Dear me! Why he's quite a fine Gentleman; I   60
thought Poets were always as poor as Job.

Mrs. Voluble. Why so they are, my dear, in common; your
real Poet is all rags & atoms: but Mr. Dabler is quite another
thing; he's what you may call a Poet of Fashion. He studies,
sometimes, by the Hour together. O he's quite one of the
great Geniusses, I assure [3v] you! I listened at his Door,
once, when when he was at it,— for he talks so loud when
he's by himself, that we can hear him quite down Stairs: but
I could make nothing out, only a heap of Words all in a
Chime, as one may say,— mean, lean, Dean, wean— Lord, I   70
can't remember half of them! At first when he came, I used
to run in his Room, & ask what was the matter? but he told
me I must not mind him, for it was only the *Fit* was on him,
I think he called it, & so—

Young Woman. I wish Somebody would shew me some Ribbons, I have waited this half Hour.

Mrs. Wheedle. O, ay, I forgot; do shew this young Gentlewoman some Ribbons. (*in a low voice.*) Take last year's.
[(*to* ***Young Woman.***)] You shall see some just out of the
loom.   80

Mrs. Voluble. Well but, Mrs. Wheedle, I was going to tell you
about Miss Stanley; you must know she's a young Lady with
a Fortune all in her own Hands, for she's just come of age, &
she's got neither Papa nor Mama, & so—

<*Enter a **Footman.***>

<***Footman.*** Lady Bab Vertigo desires Mrs. Wheedle will come
to the Coach Door.   (***Exit.***)>

<(***Mrs. Wheedle*** *goes out.*)>

---

77 *Mrs. Wheedle.*] Mrs. Wheedle. *MS*
86–87 Marked for possible excision in MS

*Mrs. **Voluble**, turning herself to Miss Jenny*. And so, Miss
Jenny, as I was [4r] saying, this young lady came to spend
the Winter in Town with Lady Smatter, & so she fell in Love
with my lady's Nephew, Mr. Beaufort, & Mr. Beaufort fell in   90
Love with her, & so—
                      *Re-enter **Mrs. Wheedle***.
Mrs. Wheedle. Miss Jenny, take Lady Bab the new Trimming.
*Mrs. **Voluble**, turning to Miss Sally*. And so, Miss Sally, the
match is all agreed upon, & they are to be married next
Week, & so, as soon as the Ceremony is over—
Mrs. Wheedle. Miss Sally, put away those Ribbons.
*Mrs. **Voluble**, turning to Miss Polly* And so, Miss Polly, as
soon as the Ceremony's over, the Bride & Bridegroom—
Censor, *within*. No, faith, not I! do you think I want to study
the fashion of a Lady's Top knot?   100
Beaufort. Nay, prithee, Censor, in compassion to me—
              *Enter **Beaufort** and **Censor** strug'ling*.
Censor. Why how now, Beaufort? is not a man's person his
own property? do you conclude that, because you take the
liberty to expose your own to a ridiculous & unmanly situa-
tion, you may use the same freedom with your Friend's?
Beaufort. Pho, prithee don't be so churlish. Pray, ma'am, (*ad-
vancing to **Mrs. Wheedle**.*) has Miss Stanley been here this
Morning?
Mrs. Wheedle. No, Sir; but I expect her every moment.[4v]
Beaufort. Then, if you'll give me leave, I'll wait till she   110
comes.
Censor. Do as you list, but, for my part, I am gone.
Beaufort. How! will you not stay with me?
Censor. No, Sir; I'm a very stupid fellow,— I take no manner
of delight in Tapes & Ribbons. I leave you, therefore, to the
unmolested contemplation of this valuable collection of
Dainties: & I doubt not but you will be equally charmed &
edified by the various curiosities you will behold, & the
sagacious observations you will hear. Sir, I heartily wish you
well entertained.   (*going*.)   120
Beaufort, *holding him*. Have you no Bowels, man?
Censor. Yes, for *myself*,— & therefore it is I leave you.

Beaufort. You sha'n't go, I swear!

Censor. With what Weapons will you stay me? Will you tie me
to your little Finger with a piece of Ribbon, like a lady's
Sparrow? or will you inthrall me in a Net of Brussel's Lace?
Will you raise a Fortification of Caps? or Barricade me with
Furbelows? Will you Fire at me a Broad Side of Pompoons?
or will you stop my retreat with a Fan?

Miss Jenny. Dear, how odd the Gentleman talks! [5r]   130

Mrs. Wheedle. I wonder they don't ask to look at something.

Mrs. Voluble. I fancy I know who they are. (*whispers.*)

Beaufort. Are you not as able to bear the place as I am? if you
had any Grace, you would Blush to be thus out-done in for-
bearance.

Censor. But, my good friend, do you not consider that there is
some little difference in our situations? I, for which I bless
my Stars! am a *Free* man, & therefore may be allowed to
have an opinion of my own, to act with consistency, & to   140
be guided by the light of Reason: you, for which I most
heartily pity you, are a Lover, &, consequently, can have no
pretensions to similar privileges. With you, therefore, the
practice of patience, the toleration of impertinence, & the
Study of nonsence, are become duties indispensable; &
where can you find more ample occasion to display these
acquirements, than in this Region of Foppery, Extravagance
& Folly?

Beaufort. Ought you not, in justice, to acknowledge some
obligation to me for introducing you to a place which   150
abounds in such copious materials to gratify your Splenetic
Humour?[5v]

Censor. obligation? what, for shewing me new Scenes of the
absurdities of my Fellow Creatures?

Beaufort. Yes, Since those new Scenes give fresh occasion to
exert that Spirit of railing which makes the whole happiness
of your Life.

---

133 (*whispers.*)] whispers. *MS*

Censor. Do you imagine, then, that, like Spencer's Strife, I
  seek occasion? Have I not Eyes? & can I open them without
  becoming a Spectator of Dissipation, Idleness, Luxury & dis-   160
  order? Have I not Ears? & can I use them without becoming
  an Auditor of Malevolence, Envy, futility & Detraction? O
  Beaufort, take me where I can *avoid* occasion of railing, &
  then, indeed, I will confess my obligation to you!

Mrs. Voluble whispering Mrs. Wheedle. It's the youngest
  that's the Bridegroom, that is to be; but I'm pretty sure I
  know the other too, for he comes to see Mr. Dabler; I'll
  speak to him. (*advances to Censor.*) Sir, your humble Servant.

Censor. Madam!   170

Mrs. Voluble. I beg your pardon, Sir, but I think I've had the
  pleasure of seeing you at my House, Sir, when you've called
  upon Mr. Dabler.

Censor. Mr. Dabler?— O, yes, I recollect.— Why, Beaufort,
  what [6r] do you mean? did you bring me hither to be food
  to this magpie?

Beaufort. Not I, upon my Honour; I never saw the Woman before. Who is she?

Censor. A Fool, a prating, intolerable Fool. Dabler Lodges at
  her House, & whoever passes through her Hall to visit him,   180
  she claims for her acquaintance. She will consume more
  Words in an Hour than Ten Men will in a Year; she is in-
  fected with a rage for talking, yet has nothing to say, which
  is a Disease of all others the most pernicious to her fellow
  Creatures, since the method she takes for her own relief

---

158 Spencer's Strife: Edmund Spenser (1552?–1599), author of *The Faerie
Queen* (1590, 1596. Ed. A.C. Hamilton. New York: Longman, 1977). In
Book II, Canto iv, Occasion (of Sin) and her child, Furor, are sought by Atin,
who represents strife, but who is not the figure Strife (199–206, 206n). See
also Charles Huntington Whitman, *A Subject Index to the Poems of Edmund
Spenser* (1919. New York: Russel & Russel, 1966), 19.

163 take me . . . *avoid* occasion of railing: reminiscent of *Satires*, I.30., by
Juvenal (A.D. 60?–130?): "It is hard not to write satire" (*Juvenal and
Persius*. The Loeb Classical Library. Trans. G.G. Ramsay. Cambridge: Har-
vard University Press, 1950, 4–5).

proves their bane. Her Tongue is as restless as Scandal, &, like that, feeds upon nothing, yet attacks & tortures every thing; & it vies, in rapidity of motion, with the circulation of the Blood in a Frog's Foot.

Miss Jenny *to Mrs Voluble.* I think the Gentleman's very   190
proud, ma'am, to answer you so short.

Mrs. Voluble. O, but he won't get off so, I can tell him! I'll speak to him again. Poor Mr. Dabler, Sir, [6v] (*to Censor.*) has been troubled with a very bad Head ache lately; I tell him he studies too much, but he says he can't help it; however, I think it's a Friend's part to advise him against it, for a little caution can do no harm, you know, Sir, if it does no good, & Mr. Dabler's such a worthy, agreeable Gentleman, & so much the Scholar, 'twould be a thousand pities he should come to any ill. Pray, Sir, do you think   200 he'll ever make a match of it with Mrs. Sapient? She's ready enough, we all know, & to be sure, for the matter of that, she's no chicken. <Pray, Sir, how old do you reckon she may be?>

Censor. <Really, Madam, I have no talents for calculating the age of a Lady.> What a torrent of Impertinence! Upon my Honour, Beaufort, if you don't draw this Woman off, I shall decamp.

Beaufort. I cannot imagine what detains Cecilia; however, I will do any thing rather than wait with such Gossips by my-   210 self. I hope, ma'am, we don't keep you standing?

Mrs. Voluble. O no, Sir, I was quite tired of sitting. What a po-lite young Gentleman, Miss Jenny! I'm sure he deserves [7r] to marry a Fortune. I'll speak to him about the 'Sprit Party; he'll be quite Surprised to find how much I know of the matter. I think, Sir, your name's Mr. Beaufort?

Beaufort. At your Service, ma'am.

Mrs. Voluble. I was pretty sure it was you, sir, for I happened to be at my Window one morning when you called in a Coach; & Mr. Dabler was out,— that is, between Friends, he   220 was only at his Studies, but he said he was out, & so that's all one. So you gave in a Card, & drove off. I hope, Sir, your

---

203-206 marked for possible excision in MS

good aunt, my Lady Smatter, is well? for though I have not
the pleasure of knowing her Ladyship myself, I know them
that do. <I suppose you two Gentlemen are always of the
'Sprit Party, at my Lady's House.>

<*Censor.* 'Sprit Party? prithee, Beaufort, what's that?>

<*Beaufort.* O, the most fantastic absurdity under Heaven. My
good aunt has established a kind of club at her House, pro-
fessedly for the discussion of literary Subjects; & the Set   230
who compose it are about as well qualified for the Purpose,
as so many dirty Cabbin Boys would be to find out the Lon-
gitude. To a very little reading, they join less Understanding,
& no Judgement, [7v] yet they decide upon Books & Authors with the most confirmed confidence in their abilities
for the Task. And this club they have had the modesty to
nominate the Esprit Party.>

Censor. Nay, when you have told me Lady Smatter is President,
you need add nothing more to convince me of it's futility.
Faith, Beaufort, were you my Enemy instead of my friend, I   240
should scarce forbear commisserating your situation in being
dependant upon that Woman. I hardly know a more insufferable Being, for having, unfortunately, just *tasted the Pierian
Spring*, she has acquired that *little knowledge*, so dangerous
to shallow understandings, which serves no other purpose
than to stimulate a display of Ignorance.

Mrs. Voluble. I always know, Sir, when there's going to be a
'Sprit party, for Mr. Dabler shuts himself up to study. Pray,
Sir, did you ever see his monody on the Birth of Miss Dan-
dle's Lap Dog?   250

Censor. A monody on a Birth?

Mrs. Voluble. Yes, Sir; a monody, or Elegy, I don't exactly
know which you call it, but I think it's one of the prettiest

---

225-237 marked for possible excision in manuscript

243-244 Alexander Pope (1688-1744), in *An Essay on Criticism* (1711),
wrote "A *little learning* is a dang'rous Thing;/Drink deep, or taste not the
Pierian Spring" (*The Poems of Alexander Pope*. Twickenham Edition. 11
vols. Gen. Ed. John Butt. New Haven: Yale University Press, 1939-1969,
1:264).

249 monody: The *Oxford English Dictionary* (hereafter *OED*) defines *monody* as a lament, dirge, or funeral oration.

things he ever wrote; there he tells us— O dear, is not that
Mrs. Sapient's Coach? I'm pretty sure I know the [8r]
Cypher.

Censor. Mrs. Sapient? Nay, Beaufort, if *She* is coming hither—

Beaufort. Patience, Man; she is one of the set, & will divert
you.

Censor. You are mistaken; such consummate folly only makes   260
me melancholy. She is more weak & superficial even than
Lady Smatter, yet she has the same facility in giving herself
credit for wisdom; & there is a degree of assurance in her
conceit that is equally wonderful & disgusting, for as Lady
Smatter, from the shallowness of her knowledge, upon all
subjects forms a *wrong* Judgement, Mrs. Sapient, from extreme weakness of parts, is incapable of forming *any*; but,
to compensate for that deficiency, she retails all the opinions she hears, & confidently utters them as her own. Yet,
in the most notorious of her plagiarisms, she affects a   270
scrupulous modesty, & apologises for troubling the Company with her poor opinion!

Beaufort. She is, indeed, immeasurably wearisome.

Censor. When she utters a truth self-evident as that the Sun
shines at noon Day, she speaks it as a Discovery resulting
from her own peculiar penetration & Sagacity.

Beaufort. Silence! she is here.

Enter Mrs. Sapient. [8v]

Mrs. Sapient. O Mrs. Wheedle, how could you disappoint me
so of my short apron? I believe you make it a rule never to
keep to your Time; & I declare, for *my* part, I know nothing   280
so provoking as people's promising more than they perform.

Mrs. Wheedle. Indeed, ma'am, I beg ten thousand pardons,
but really, ma'am, we've been so hurried, that upon my
Word, ma'am— but you shall certainly have it this after-
noon. Will you give me leave to shew you any Caps, ma'am?
I have some exceeding pretty ones just finished.

Mrs. Sapient, looking at the Caps. O, for Heaven's sake, don't
shew me such flaunting things, for, in *my* opinion, nothing
can be really elegant that is Tawdry.   290

265-266 upon all Subjects] *inserted to replace one indecipherable word*

Mrs. Wheedle. But here, ma'am, is one I'm sure you'll like; it's
in the immediate Taste,— only look at it, ma'am! what can
be prettier?

Mrs. Sapient. Why yes, this is well enough, only I'm afraid it's
too young for me; don't you think it is?

Mrs. Wheedle. Too young? dear ma'am no, I'm sure it will become you of all things: only try it. (*Holds it over her Head.*)
O ma'am, you can't think how charmingly you look in it! & it
sets so sweetly! I never saw any thing so becoming in my life.

Mrs. Sapient. Is it? well, I think I'll have it,— if you are [9r]   300
sure it is not too young for me. You must know, I am might-
ily for people's consulting their Time of Life in their choice
of Cloaths: &, in *my* opinion, there is a wide difference between fifteen & fifty.

Censor, *to Beaufort.* She'll certainly tell us, next, that, in *her*
opinion, a man who has but one Eye, would look rather better if he had another!

Mrs. Wheedle. O I'm sure, ma'am, you'll be quite in love with
this Cap, when you see how well you look in it. Shall I shew
you some of our new Ribbons, ma'am?   310

Mrs. Sapient. O, I know, now, you want to tempt me; but *I* always say the best way to escape temptation is to run away
from it: however, as I *am* here—

Mrs. Voluble. Had not you better sit down, ma'am?

                                        (*offering a chair.*)

Mrs. Sapient. O Mrs. Voluble, is it you? How do do? Lord, I
don't like any of these Ribbons. Pray how does Mr. Dabler do?

Mrs. Voluble. Very well, thank you, ma'am; that is, not *very*
well, but *pretty* well considering, for to be sure, ma'am, so
much study's very bad for the Health; it's pity he don't take
more care of himself, & so I often tell him; but your great   320
Wits never mind what little folks say, [9v] if they talk never
so well, & I'm sure I've sometimes talked to him by the Hour
together about it, for I'd never spare my words to serve a
friend; however, it's all to no purpose, for he says he has a
kind of a *Fury*, I think he calls it, upon him, that makes him

---

316 Mr. Dabler] M: Dabler *MS*
317 *Mrs. Voluble.*] Mrs. Voluble. *MS*

write whether he will or not. And, to be sure, he does write
most charmingly! & he has such a collection of Miniscrips!
Lord, I question if a pastry Cook or a Cheesemonger could
use them in a Year! for he says he never destroyed a Line he
ever wrote in his life. All that he don't like, he tells me he   330
Keeps by him for his Postimus works, as he calls them, &
I've some notion he intends soon to print them.

Mrs. Wheedle. Do, ma'am, pray let me put this Cloak up for
you, & I'll make you a Hat for it immediately.

Mrs. Sapient. Well, then, take great care how you put in the
Ribbon, for you know I won't keep it if it does not please
me. Mr. Beaufort!— Lord bless me, how long have you been
here? O Heavens! is that Mr. Censor? I can scarce believe my
Eyes! Mr. Censor in a Milliner's Shop! Well, this does, indeed, justify an observation I have often made, that the   340
greatest Geniusses sometimes do the oddest things. [10r]

Censor. Your surprise, madam, at seeing me here to-Day will
bear no comparison to what I must myself experience,
should you ever see me here again.

Mrs. Sapient. O, I know well how much you must despise all
this sort of Business, &, I assure you, I am equally averse to
it myself: indeed I often think what pity it is so much Time
should be given to mere shew;— for what are we the better
to-morrow for what we have worn to Day? No Time, in *my*
opinion, turns to so little account as that which we spend in   350
Dress.

Censor, to Beaufort. Did you ever hear such an impudent
falsehood?

Mrs. Sapient. For *my* part, I always wear just what the
Milliner & Mantua-maker please to send me; for I have a
kind of maxim upon this Subject which has some weight
with *me*, though I don't know if any body else ever suggested it: but it is, that the real value of a Person Springs

---

328 Pastry Cook or Cheesemonger: Old paper was often used to wrap
cheese or to line baking pans. In the eighteenth century, John Warburton
(1682-1759) had a cook who is said to have destroyed the manuscripts of
some plays by Shakespeare in this manner. See John Freehafer, "John Warburton's Lost Plays" (*Studies in Bibliography* 23 (1970): 154-162).

from the *mind*, not from the outside appearance. So I never
trouble myself to look at anything till the moment I put it   360
on. Be sure (*turning quick to the Milliners,*) you take care
how you trim the Hat! I sha'n't wear it else.

Censor. Prithee, Beaufort, how long will you give a man [10v]
to decide which is greatest, her folly, or her Conceit?

Mrs. Sapient. Gentlemen, good morning; Mrs. Voluble, you
may give my Compliments to Mr. Dabler. Mrs. Wheedle,
pray send the things in Time, for, to *me*, nothing is more
disagreeable than to be disappointed.

As she is going out, Jack enters abruptly, & brushes past her.

Mrs. Sapient. O Heavens!

Jack. Lord, ma'am, I beg you a thousand pardons! I did not see   370
you, I declare. I hope I did not hurt you?

Mrs. Sapient. No, Sir, no; but you a little alarmed me,— & really an alarm, when one does not know how to account for
it, gives one a rather odd Sensation,— at least *I* find it so.

Jack. Upon my Word, ma'am, I'm very sorry,— I'm sure if I'd
seen you— but I was in such monstrous haste, I had no
Time to look about me.

Mrs. Sapient. O, Sir, 'tis of no consequence; yet, allow me to
observe that, in *my* opinion, too much haste generally de-
feats it's own purpose. Sir, good morning.   (*Exit.*)   380

Beaufort. Why Jack, won't you see her to her Coach?

Jack. O ay, true, so I must!   (*follows her.*)

Censor. This Brother of yours, Beaufort, is a most ingenious
youth. [11r]

Beaufort. He has foibles which you, I am sure, will not spare;
but he means well, & is extremely good-natured.

Censor. Nay, but I am serious, for, without ingenuity, no man,
I think, could continue to be always in a hurry, who is never
employed.

Re-enter Jack.

Jack. Plague take it, Brother, how unlucky it was that you   390
made me go after her! in running up to her, my duced spurs
caught hold of some of her falaldrums, & in my haste to dis-
engage myself, I tore off half her trimming. She went off in a

---

363-364 give a man / to decide] ~ man [catchword to] / decide *MS*

very ill-humour, telling me that, in *her* opinion, a disagreeable accident was very— very— very disagreeable, I think,
or something to that purpose.

Beaufort. But, for Heaven's Sake, Jack, what is the occasion of
all this furious haste?

Jack. Why Lord, you know I'm always in a hurry; I've no notion of Dreaming away Life: how the Deuce is any thing to   400
be done without a little spirit?

Beaufort. Pho, prithee, Jack, give up this idle humour.

Jack. Idle? nay, Brother, call me what else you please, but you
can never charge me with idleness.

Beaufort. Why, with all your boasted activity, I question if
there is a man in England who would be more embarrassed
how to give any account of his Time. [11v]

Jack. Well, well, I can't stay now to discourse upon these matters,— I have too many things to *do*, to stand here talking.

Beaufort. Nay, don't go till you tell us what you have to do   410
this morning?

Jack. Why more things than either of you would do in a
month, but I can't stop now to tell you any of them, for I
have 3 friends waiting for me in Hyde Park, & 20 places to
call at in my way.   (*going.*)

Mrs. Wheedle, following him. Sir would you not chuse to
look at some Ruffles?

Jack. O, ay,— have you any thing new? what do you call these?

Mrs. Wheedle. O pray, Sir, take care! they are so delicate
they'll hardly bear to be touched.   420

Jack. I don't like them at all! shew me some others.

Mrs. Wheedle. Why, sir, only see! you have quite Spoilt this
pair.

Jack. Have I? well, then, you must put them up for me. But
pray have you got no better?

Mrs. Wheedle. I'll look some directly, Sir,— but, dear sir, pray
don't put your Switch upon the Caps! I hope you'll excuse
me, Sir, but the set is all in all in these little tasty things.

Censor. And pray, Jack, are all your hurries equally important,
& equally necessary as those of this morning?   430

---

430 as] *cor*, with *or*

Jack. Lord, you grave fellows, who plod on from Day to Day without any notion of Life & Spirit, spend half your Lives [12r] in asking people questions they don't know how to answer.

Censor. And we might consume the other half to as little purpose, if we waited to find out questions which such people *do* know how to answer.

Jack. Severe, very severe, that! however, I have not Time, now, for Repartee, but I shall give you a Rowland for your Oliver when we meet again.   (*going.*)   440

Mrs. Wheedle. Sir I've got the Ruffles,— won't you look at them?

Jack. O, the Ruffles! well, I'm glad you've found them, but I can't stay to look at them now. Keep them in the way against I call again.   (*Exit.*)

Mrs. Wheedle. Miss Jenny, put these Ruffles up again. That Gentleman never knows his own mind.

Miss Jenny. I'm sure he's tumbled & tossed the things about like mad.

Censor. 'Tis to be much regretted, Beaufort, that such a youth   450
as this was not an Elder Brother.

Beaufort. Why so?

Censor. Because the next Heir might so easily get rid of him; for, if he was knocked down, I believe he would think it loss of Time to get up again, & if he were pushed into a River, I question if he would not be Drowned, ere he could persuade himself to swim long enough in the same Direction to save himself.

Beaufort. He is young, & I hope this ridiculous humour will wear away. [12v]   460

Censor. But how came *you* so wholly to escape it's infection? I find not, in you, any portion of this inordinate desire of action, to which all power of thinking must be sacrificed.

439–440 Rowland for your Oliver: Derived from the medieval romances concerning Charlemagne and his Paladins, the most famous of whom is Roland. Roland and Oliver became friends after a prolonged combat, the winner of which could not be determined. The phrase "Roland for an Oliver" thus came to mean verbal combat, in which "[one gives] as good as one gets" (*OED*).

Beaufort. Why we are but half Brothers, & our Educations
were as different as our Fathers, for my mother's Second
Husband was no more like her first, than am *I to Her-*
cules;— though Jack, indeed, has no resemblance even to
his own Father.

Censor. Resemblance? an Hare & a Tortoise are not more different; for Jack is always running, without knowing what he   470
pursues, & his Father is always pondering, without knowing
what he thinks of.

Beaufort. The Truth is, Mr. Codger's humour of perpetual de-
liberation so early sickened his Son, that the fear of inherit-
ing any share of it, made him rush into the opposite extreme, & determine to avoid the censure of inactive
meditation, by executing every plan he could form at the
very moment of Projection.

Censor. And pray, Sir,— if such a Question will not endanger
a challenge,— what think you, by this Time, of the punctu-   480
ality of your Mistress?

Beaufort. Why,— to own the truth— I fear I must have made
some mistake.

Censor. Bravo, Beaufort! ever doubt your own Senses, in preference to suspecting your mistress of negligence or Caprice.

Beaufort. She is much too noble minded, too just in her sentiments, & too uniform in her conduct, to be guilty of either.
[13r]

Censor. Bravissimo, Beaufort! I commend your patience, &,
this Time twelvemonth I'll ask you how it wears! In the   490
mean Time, however, I would not upon any account interrupt your contemplations either upon her Excellencies, or
your own mistakes, but, as I expect no advantage from the
one, you must excuse my any longer suffering from the
other: &, ere you again entangle me in such a wilderness of
frippery, I shall take the liberty more closely to investigate
the accuracy of your appointments.   (*Exit.*)

Beaufort. My Situation begins to grow as ridiculous as it is disagreeable; Surely Cecilia cannot have forgotten me!

466-467 *I to Hercules*: In *Hamlet* (1602) by William Shakespeare (1564-
1616), Hamlet describes his uncle, Claudius, as being "no more like my fa-
ther/ Than I to Hercules" (1.2. 152-153. *Riverside Shakespeare*, 1145).

Mrs Voluble *advancing to him.* To be sure, Sir, it's vastly in-   500
commodious to be kept waiting so, but, sir, if I might put in
a Word, I think—

Enter Jack running.

Jack. Lord, Brother, I quite forgot to tell you Miss Stanley's
message.

Beaufort. Message! What message?

Jack. I declare I had got half way to Hyde Park, before I ever
thought of it.

Beaufort. Upon my Honour, Jack, this is too much!

Jack. Why I ran back the moment I recollected it, & what could I
do more? I would not even stop to tell Will. Scamper what was   510
the matter, so he has been calling & bawling after [13v]me all
the way I came. I gave him the slip when I got to the shop,—
but I'll just step & see if he's in the street.   (*going.*)

Beaufort. Jack, you'll provoke me to more anger than you are
prepared for! what was the message? tell me quickly!

Jack. O ay, true! why she said she could not come.

Beaufort. Not come? but *why*? I'm sure she told you *why*?

Jack. O yes, she told me a long story about it,— but I've forgot
what it was.

Beaufort, *warmly.* Recollect, then!   520

Jack. Why so I will. O, it was all your aunt Smatter's fault,—
somebody came in with the new Ranelagh Songs, so she
stayed at Home to study them; & Miss Stanley bid me say
she was very sorry, but she could not come by herself.

Beaufort. And why might I not have been told this sooner?

Jack. Why she desired me to come & tell you of it an Hour or
2 ago, but I had so many places to stop at by the way, I
could not possibly get here sooner: & when I came, my
Head was so full of my own appointments, that I never once

<hr/>

522 Ranelagh Songs: The Ranelagh Gardens in Chelsea had a famous rotunda
in which an orchestra played and noted singers performed: Rosamond
Bayne-Powell, *Eighteenth-Century London Life* (New York: E.P. Dutton,
1938), 149.

524 . . . come by herself: Proper young unmarried women never went out
without a chaperone (Bayne-Powell, *Eighteenth-Century London Life,* 69);
otherwise, they might be accosted by rakes.

thought of her message. However, I must run back to Will.   530
Scamper, or he'll think me crazy.

Beaufort. Hear me, Jack! if you do not take pains to correct
this absurd rage to attempt every thing, while you execute
nothing, you will render yourself as contemptible to the
World, as you are useless or mischievous to your Family.
                                                    (***Exit.***)

Jack. What a passion he's in! I've a good mind to run to Miss
Stanley, & beg her to intercede for me.   (*going.*) [14r]

Mrs. Wheedle. Sir, won't you please to look at the Ruffles?

Jack. O ay, true,— where are they?

Mrs. Wheedle. Here, Sir. Miss Jenny, give me those Ruffles   540
again.

Jack. O if they a'n't ready, I can't stay.   (***Exit.***)

Mrs. Voluble. Well, Mrs. Wheedle, I'm sure you've a pleasant
life of it here, in seeing so much of the World. I'd a great
mind to have spoke to that young Gentleman, for I'm pretty
sure I've seen him before, though I can't tell where. But he
was in such a violent hurry, I could not get in a word. He's a
fine lively young Gentleman, to be sure. But now, Mrs.
Wheedle, when will you come & Drink a Snug dish of Tea
with me? you, & Miss Jenny, & any of the young ladies that   550
can be spared? I'm sure if you can *all* come—

Enter Bob.

Bob. I ask pardon, Ladies & Gentlemen, but pray is my mother
here?

Mrs. Voluble. What's that to you, sirrah? who gave you leave
to follow me? get Home, directly, you dirty figure you! go,
go, I say!

Bob. Why Lord, mother, you've been out all the morning, &
never told Betty what was for Dinner!

Mrs. Voluble. Why you great, Tall, greedy, gormondising, lub-
berly Cub, you, what signifies whether you have any Dinner   560
or no? go, get away, you idle, good for nothing, dirty,
greasy, hulking, tormenting—

she drives him off, & the
scene closes.

End of Act the first. [14v]

Act II.

Scene, a Drawing Room at Lady Smatter's.
Lady Smatter & Cecilioa.

Lady Smatter. Yes, yes, this song is certainly Mr. Dabler's, I am not to be deceived in his style. What say you, my dear Miss Stanley, don't you think I have found him out.

Cecilia. Indeed I am too little acquainted with his Poems to be able to judge.

Lady Smatter. Your indifference surprises me! for my part, I am never at rest till I have discovered the authors of every thing that comes out; &, indeed, I commonly hit upon them in a moment. I declare I sometimes wonder at myself, when I think how lucky I am in my guesses.   10

Cecilia. Your Ladyship devotes so much Time to these researches, that it would be strange if they were unsuccessful.

Lady Smatter. Yes, I do indeed devote my Time to them; I own it without blushing, for how, as a certain author Says, can Time be better employed than in cultivating intellectual accomplishments? And I am often Surprised, my dear Miss Stanley, that a young lady of your good sense should not be more warmly engaged in the same pursuit. [2r]

Cecilia. My pursuits, whatever they may be, are too unimpor-   20
tant to deserve being made public.

Lady Smatter. Well to be sure, we are all Born with sentiments of our own, as I read in a Book I can't just now recol-

---

6–10 When *Evelina* was published anonymously, people tried to attribute it to writers as diverse as Horace Walpole and Hester Thrale, and Sir Joshua Reynolds offered a reward of fifty pounds to the person who would tell him the name of the author. Even after the secret was discovered, some had difficulty believing that *Evelina* could be the unaided work of a young woman.

48

lect the name of, so I ought not to wonder that yours &
mine do not coincide; for, I declare, if my pursuits were
not made public, I should not have any at all, for where can
be the pleasure of reading Books, & studying authors, if
one is not to have the credit of talking of them?

Cecilia. Your Ladyship's desire of celebrity is too well known
for your motives to be doubted.   30

Lady Smatter. Well but, my dear Miss Stanley, I have been
thinking for some Time past of your becoming a member of
our Esprit Party: Shall I put up your name?

Cecilia. By no means; my ambition aspires not at an Honour
for which I feel myself so little qualified.

Lady Smatter. Nay, but you are too modest; you can't suppose how much you may profit by coming among us. I'll
tell you some of our regulations. The principal persons of
our party are Authors & Critics; the authors always bring us
something new of their own, & the Critics regale us with   40
manuscript notes upon something old.

Cecilia. And in what class is your Ladyship?

Lady Smatter. O, I am among the Critics. I love criticism [2v]
passionately, though it is really laborious Work, for it
obliges one to read with a vast deal of attention. I declare I
am sometimes so immensely fatigued with the toil of studying for faults & objections, that I am ready to fling all my
Books behind the Fire.

Cecilia. And what authors have you chiefly criticised?

Lady Smatter. Pope & Shakespeare. I have found more errors   50
in those than in any other.

Cecilia. I hope, however, for the sake of readers less fastidi-
ous, your Ladyship has also left them some beauties.

Lady Smatter. O yes, I have not cut them up regularly
through; indeed I have not, yet, read above half their
Works, so how they will fare as I go on, I can't determine.
O, here's Beaufort.

Enter Beaufort.

Beaufort. Your Ladyship's most obedient.

Cecilia. Mr. Beaufort, I am quite ashamed to see You! yet the
disappointment I occasioned you was as involuntary on my   60

part, as it could possibly be disagreeable on yours. Your
Brother, I hope, prevented your waiting long?

Beaufort. That you meant he should is sufficient reparation
for my loss of Time; but what must be the [3r] disappointment that an apology from you would not soften?

Lady Smatter, *reading.* O lovely, charming, beauteous
maid,— I wish this Song was not so difficult to get by
Heart,— but I am always beginning one Line for another.
After all, Study is a most fatiguing thing! O how little does
the World suspect, when we are figuring in all the bril-   70
liancy of Conversation, the private hardships, & secret
labours of a Belle Esprit!

Enter a Servant.

Servant. Mr. Codger, my lady.

Enter Mr. Codger.

Lady Smatter. Mr. Codger, your Servant. I hope I see you well?

Codger. Your Ladyship's most humble. Not so well, indeed,
as I could wish, yet, perhaps, better than I deserve to be.

Lady Smatter. How is my friend Jack?

Codger. I can't directly say, madam; I have not seen him
these 2 Hours, & poor Jack is but a harem scarem young
man; many things may have happened to him in the Space   80
of 2 Hours.

Lady Smatter. And what, my good Sir, can you apprehend?

Codger. To enumerate all the Casualties I apprehend might,
perhaps, be tedious, I will, therefore, only mention the
Heads. In the first place, he may be thrown from [3v] his
Horse; in the 2ᵈ place, he may be run over while on Foot; in
the 3ᵈ place—

Lady Smatter. O pray *place* him no more in situations so horrible. Have you heard lately from our friends in the north?

Codger. Not very lately, madam: the last Letter I received was   90
Dated the 16ᵗʰ of February, & that, you know, madam, was
5 Weeks last Thursday.

Lady Smatter. I hope you had good news?

Codger. Why, madam, yes; at least, none bad. My Sister Debo-

---

77 If Beaufort is Smatter's nephew, and Jack is merely her friend, then Beaufort is related to Smatter on his father's side.

rah acquainted me with many curious little pieces of History that have happened in her neighbourhood: would it be
agreeable to your Ladyship to hear them?

Lady Smatter. O no, I would not take up so much of your Time.

Codger. I cannot, madam, employ my Time more agreeably.
Let me see,— in the first place— no, that was not first,—   100
let me recollect!

Beaufort. Pray, Sir, was any mention made of Tom?

Codger. Yes; but don't be impatient; I shall speak of him in
his turn.

Beaufort. I beg your pardon, Sir, but I enquired from hearing
he was not well.

Codger. I shall explain whence that report arose in [4r] a few
minutes; in the mean Time, I must beg you not to interrupt
me, for I am trying to arrange a chain of anecdotes for the
satisfaction of Lady Smatter.   110

Lady Smatter. Bless me, Mr. Codger, I did not mean to give
you so much trouble.

Codger. It will be no trouble in the World, if your Ladyship will,
for a while, forbear speaking to me, though the loss upon the
occasion will be all mine. (*He retires to the Side Scene.*)

Lady Smatter. What a formal old Fogrum the man grows!
Beaufort, have you seen this Song?

Beaufort. I believe not, madam.

Lady Smatter. O, it's the prettiest thing! but I don't think
you have a true taste for Poetry; I never observed you to be   120
enraptured, lost in Extacy, or hurried as it were out of yourself, when I have been reading to you. But *my* enthusiasm
for poetry may, perhaps, carry me too far; come now, my
dear Miss Stanley, be sincere with me, don't you think I indulge this propensity too much?

---

107 in / a few] in [*catchword* a] / in a few *MS*

116 Fogrum: an "antiquated or old-fashioned person, a fogy" (*OED*).

124-25 Don't you think I indulge this propensity too much?: Burney once
described her own pursuits, saying "So early was I impressed myself with
ideas that fastened degradation to [writing fiction], that . . . I struggled
against the propensity . . . which had impelled me into its toils" (*The Wanderer*, xx-xxi).

Cecilia. I should be sorry to have your Ladyship suppose me
  quite insensible to the elegance of Literary pursuits, though
  I niether claim any Title, nor profess any ability to judge of
  them.

Lady Smatter. O You'll do very well in a few Years. But, as   130
  you observe, I own I think there is something rather [4v] elegant in a Taste for these sort of amusements: otherwise,
  indeed, I should not have taken so much pains to acquire
  it, for, to confess the truth, I had from Nature quite an aver-
  sion to reading,— I remember the Time when the very
  Sight of a Book was disgustful to me!

Codger *coming forward.* I believe, madam, I can now satisfy
  your enquiries.

Lady Smatter. What enquiries?

Codger. Those your Ladyship made in relation to my Letter   140
  from our Friends in Yorkshire. In the first place, my Sister
  Deborah writes me Word that the new Barn which, you
  may remember, was begun last Summer, is pretty nearly finished. And here, in my Pocket Book, I have gotten the Dimensions of it. It is 15 Feet by—

Lady Smatter. O, for Heaven's Sake, Mr. Codger, don't trouble yourself to be so circumstantial.

Codger. The trouble, madam, is inconsiderable, or, if it were
  otherwise, for the information of your Ladyship I would
  most readily go through with it. It is 15 Feet by 30. And   150
  pray does your Ladyship remember the Old Dog Kennel at
  the Parsonage House?

Lady Smatter. No, Sir; I never look at Dog Kennels.

Codger. Well, madam, my Sister Deborah writes me Word—
                          Enter Servant.

Servant. Mr. Dabler, my lady. [5r]
                          Enter Mr. Dabler.

Lady Smatter. Mr. Dabler, you are the man in the World I
  most wished to see.

Dabler. Your Ladyship is Beneficence itself!

Lady Smatter. A visit from you, Mr. Dabler, is the greatest of
  favours, since your Time is not only precious to yourself,   160
  but to the World.

------
150 through] though *MS*

Dabler. It is, indeed, precious to myself, madam, when I devote it to the Service of your Ladyship. Miss Stanley, may I
hope you are as well as you look? if so, your Health must indeed be in a State of perfection; if not, never before did
Sickness wear so fair a Mask.

Lady Smatter. 'Tis a thousand pities, Mr. Dabler, to throw
away such poetical thoughts & Imagery in common Conversation.

Dabler. Why, ma'am, the truth is, something a little out of the   170
usual path is expected from a Man whom the World has
been pleased to style a Poet;— though I protest I never
knew why!

Lady Smatter. How true is it that Modesty, as Pope, or Swift,
I forget which, has it, is the constant attendant upon
Merit!

Dabler. If Merit, madam, were but the constant attendant
upon Modesty, then, indeed, I might hope to attain no little
share! Faith, I'll set that down. (*He takes out his Tablets.*)

Codger. And so, madam, my Sister Deborah writes me   180
Word— [5v]

Lady Smatter. O dear, Mr. Codger, I merely wanted to know
if all our friends were well.

Codger. Nay, if your Ladyship does not want to hear about
the Dog Kennel—

Lady Smatter. Not in the least! I hate Kennels, & Dogs too.

Codger. As you please, madam! (*aside.*) She has given me the
trouble of 10 minutes recollection, & now she won't hear
me!

Lady Smatter. Mr. Dabler, I believe I've had the pleasure of   190
seeing something of yours this morning.

Dabler. Of mine? you alarm me beyond measure!

Lady Smatter. Nay, nay, 'tis in Print, so don't be frightened.

Dabler. Your Ladyship relieves me: but, really, people are so
little delicate in taking Copies of my foolish manuscripts,

175-76 Modesty . . . . . Merit: Neither Pope nor Swift wrote this, and the attribution is probably humorous, as neither man was exactly modest. However, a close parallel occurs in *The Spectator*, no. 350, written in 1712 by Sir
Richard Steele (1672-1729): "Modesty is the certain Indication of a great
Spirit" (3: 303-304).

that I protest I go into no House without the fear of meeting something of my own. But what may it be?

Lady Smatter. Why I'll repeat it.

    O Sweetest, Softest, gentlest maid—

Dabler. No, ma'am, no;— you mistake,—   200

    O lovely, beauteous, charming maid,— is it not so?

Lady Smatter. Yes, yes, that's it. O what a vile memory is mine! after all my studying to make such a mistake! I declare I forget as fast as I learn. I shall begin to fancy myself a Wit by & by.[6r]

Dabler. Then will your Ladyship for the *first* Time be the *last* to learn Some thing. (*aside.*) 'Gad, I'll put that into an Epigram!

Lady Smatter. I was reading, the other Day, that the memory of a Poet should be short, that his Works may be original.   210

Dabler. Heavens, madam, where did you meet with that?

Lady Smatter. I can't exactly say, but either in Pope or Swift.

Dabler. O curse it, how unlucky!

Lady Smatter. Why so?

Dabler. Why, madam, 'tis my own thought! I've just finished an Epigram upon that very Subject! I protest I shall grow more and more sick of Books every Day, for I can never look into any, but I'm sure of popping upon something of my own.

Lady Smatter. Well but, dear Sir, pray let's hear your Epigram.

Dabler. Why,— if your Ladyship insists upon it—   220

    (*reads.*) Ye gentle Gods, O hear me plead,
            And Kindly grant this little loan;
            Make me forget whate'er I read
            That what I write may be my own.

209-12 the memory . . . original.] Pope did not write it. Jonathan Swift (1667-1745), in section VI of *A Tale Of A Tub* (1704), suggested the opposite, writing, ". . . *memory*, being an employment of the mind upon things past, is a faculty for which the learned in our age, have no manner of occasion . . . . upon which account we think it highly reasonable to produce our great forgetfulness, as an argument unanswerable for our great wit" (*The Prose Works of Jonathan Swift*, 14 vols. ed. Herbert John Davis [Oxford: Basil Blackwell, 1948-1975], 1: 84).

Lady Smatter. O charming! very clever indeed.

Beaufort. But pray, Sir, if such is your wish, why should you read at all?

Dabler. Why, Sir, one must read; one's reputation requires it; for it would be cruelly confusing to be asked after such or such an author, & never to have looked into him. especially to a person who passes for having some little [6v] knowledge in these matters.

Beaufort. (*aside.*) What a shallow Coxcomb!

Lady Smatter. You must positively let me have a Copy of that Epigram, Mr. Dabler. Don't you think it charming, Mr. Codger?

Codger. Madam, I never take any thing in at first hearing; if Mr. Dabler will let me have it in my own Hand, I will give your Ladyship my opinion of it, after I have read it over 2 or 3 Times.

Dabler. Sir it is much at your Service; but I must insist upon it that you don't get it by Heart.

Codger. Bless me, Sir, I should not do that in half a year! I have no turn for such sort of things.

Lady Smatter. I know not in what Mr. Dabler most excells, Epigrams, Sonnets, Odes or Elegies.

Dabler. Dear ma'am, mere nonsense! but I believe your Ladyship forgets my little Lampoons?

Lady Smatter. O no, that I never can! there you are indeed perfect.

Dabler. Your Ladyship far over-rates my poor abilities;— my Writings are mere trifles, & I believe the World would be never the worse, if they were all committed to the Flames.

Beaufort. (*aside.*) I would I could try the Experiment!

Lady Smatter. Your Talents are really Universal.

Dabler. O ma'am, you quite over-power me! but now you are pleased to mention the Word *Universal*,— did your [7r] Ladyship ever meet with my little attempt in the Epic way?

Lady Smatter. O no, you sly Creature! but I shall now suspect you of every thing.

Dabler. Your Ladyship is but too partial. I have, indeed, some little facility in Stringing Rhymes, but I should suppose there's nothing very extraordinary in that: every body, I be-

230

240

250

260

lieve, has some little Talent,— mine happens to be for Poetry, but it's all a chance! nobody can chuse for himself, &
really, to be candid, I don't know if some other things are
not of equal consequence.

Lady Smatter. There, Mr. Dabler, I must indeed differ from
you! what in the Universe can be put in competition with
Poetry?   270

Dabler. Your Ladyship's enthusiasm for the fine arts—

Enter a Servant.

Servant. Mrs. Sapient, Madam.

Lady Smatter. Lord, how tiresome! She'll talk us to Death!

Enter Mrs. Sapient.

Dear Mrs. Sapient, this is vastly good of you!

Dabler. Your arrival, madam, is particularly critical at this
Time, for we are engaged in a literary Controversy; & to
whom can we so properly apply to enlighten our Doubts
by the Sun Beams of her Counsel, as to Mrs. Sapient?

Lady Smatter. What a Sweet Speech! (*aside.*) I wonder how
he could make it to that Stupid Woman! [7v]   280

Mrs. Sapient. You do me too much Honour, Sir. But what is
the Subject I have been so unfortunate as to interrupt? for
though I shall be ashamed to offer my Sentiments before
such a Company as this, I yet have rather a peculiar way of
thinking upon this subject.

Dabler. As how, ma'am?

Mrs. Sapient. Why, Sir, it seems to *me* that a proper degree of
Courage is preferable to a superfluous excess of modesty.

Dabler. Excellent! extremely right, madam. The present question is upon Poetry. We were considering whether, impar-   290
tially Speaking, some other things are not of equal importance?

Mrs. Sapient. I am unwilling, Sir, to decide upon so delicate
a point; yet, were I to offer my humble opinion, it would
be, that though to *me* nothing is more delightful than poetry, I yet fancy there may be other things of greater utility
in common Life.

Dabler. Pray, Mr. Codger, what is your opinion?

Codger. Sir I am so intently employed in considering this Epigram, that I cannot, just now, maturely weigh your Ques-   300

tion; & indeed, Sir, to acknowledge the truth, I could have
excused your interrupting me.

Dabler. Sir you do my foolish Epigram much Honour. (*aside.*)
That Man has twice the Sense one would suppose from his
look. I'll shew him my new Sonnet. [8r]

Mrs. Sapient. How much was I surprised, Mr. Beaufort, at
seeing Mr. Censor this morning in a Milliner's Shop!

Cecilia. I rejoice to hear you had such a Companion; & yet,
perhaps, I ought rather to regret it, since the Sting of his
rallery might but inflame your disappointment & vexation.   310

Beaufort. The Sting of a professed Satirest only proves poiso-
nous to fresh Subjects; those who have often felt it are
merely tickled by the Wound.

Dabler. (*aside.*) How the Deuce shall I introduce the Sonnet?
[*to the Company.*] Pray, Ladies & Gentlemen, you who so
often visit the Muses, is there any thing new in the Poetical
way?

Lady Smatter. Who, Mr. Dabler, can so properly answer that
Question as you,— you, to whom all their Haunts are open?

Dabler. O dear ma'am, Such Compositions as mine are the   320
merest Baubles in the World! I dare say there are people
who would even be ashamed to set their names to them.

Beaufort. (*aside.*) I hope there is but one Person who would
not!

Mrs. Sapient. How much more amiable in *my* Eyes is Genius
when joined with Diffidence, than with conceit!

Codger, *returning the Epigram.* Sir I give you my thanks: & I
think, Sir, your wish is some what uncommon.

Dabler. I am much pleased, Sir, that you approve of it.
(*aside.*) This man does not want Understanding, with all   330
his formality. He'll be prodigiously struck with my sonnet.
[8v]

Mrs. Sapient. What, is that something new of Mr. Dabler's?
surely, Sir, you must Write Night & Day.

Dabler. O dear no, ma'am, for I compose with a facility that is
really surprising. yet, sometimes, to be sure, I have been

334 ma'am] maam *MS*

pretty hard Worked; in the Charade Season I protest I
hardly Slept a Wink! I spent whole Days in looking over
Dictionaries for Words of double meaning: & really I made
some not amiss. But 'twas too easy; I soon grew sick of it.   340
yet I never quite gave it up till, accidentally, I heard a
House maid say to a Scullion, "My first, is yourself; my Second, holds good chear; & my third, is my own office;"— &,
'Gad, the Word was scrub-bing!

Codger. With respect, Sir, to that point concerning which
you consulted me, I am inclined to think—

Dabler. Sir!

Codger. You were speaking to me, Sir, respecting the utility
of Poetry; I am inclined to think—

Dabler. O, apropos, now I think of it, I have a little sonnet   350
here that is quite pat to the subject, &—

Codger. What subject, good sir?

Dabler. What subject?— why— this subject, you know.

Codger. As yet, Sir, we are talking of no subject; I was going—

Dabler. Well but— ha! ha!— it puts me so in mind of this little sonnet we were speaking of, that—

Codger. But, Sir, you have not heard what I was going to
say.— [9r]

Dabler. True, Sir, true;— I'll put the Poem away for the present,— unless, indeed, you very much wish to see it?   360

Codger. Another Time will do as well, Sir. I don't rightly comprehend what I read before Company.

Dabler. Dear Sir, such trifles as these are hardly worth your
serious study; however, if you'll promise not to take a

337-38 Charades were played with teams, each of which might enact several silent tableaux in order to represent the syllables of the word in question.

342-343 Scullion, "My ~ office;"] Scullion My ~ office; *MS*

344 Samuel Johnson (1709-84), in *A Dictionary of the English Language*
(1755. rpt. New York: AMS Press, 1967), defines *scrub* as "(1) A mean fellow, either as he is supposed to scrub himself for an itch, or as he is employed in the mean offices of scouring away dirt. (2) Any thing mean or despicable. (3) A worn out broom." *Bing* is a variant of *bin*, used in the sense
of a wine bin (*OED*), which would, of course, hold "good chear."

Copy, I think I'll venture to trust you with the manuscript,— but you must be sure not to shew it a single
Soul,— & pray take great care of it.

Codger. Good Sir, I don't mean to take it at all.

Dabler. Sir!

Codger. I have no Time for reading; & I hold that these sort   370
of things only turn one's Head from matters of more importance.

Dabler. O very well, sir,— if you don't want to see it—
(*aside.*) what a tastless old Dolt! curse me if I shall hardly
be civil to him when I meet him next!

Codger. Notwithstanding which, Sir, if I should find an odd
Hour or two in the course of the Winter, I will let you
know, & you may send it to me.

Dabler. Dear Sir, you do me a vast favour! (*aside.*) The fellow's a perfect Driveler!   380

Lady Smatter. I declare, Mr. Codger, had we known you
were so indifferent to the charms of Poetry, we should
never have admitted you of our Party.

Codger. Madam I was only moved to enter it in order [9v] to
oblige your Ladyship; but I shall hardly attend it above once
more,— or twice at the utmost.

Enter Jack.

Jack to Lady Smatter. Ma'am your Servant. Where's Miss
Stanley? I'm so out of Breath I can hardly Speak. Miss Stanley, I'm come on purpose to tell you some news.

Cecilia. It ought to be of some importance by your haste.   390

Beaufort. Not a whit the more for that! his haste indicates
nothing, for it accompanies him in every thing.

Jack. Nay, if you won't hear me at once, I'm gone!

Codger. And pray, Son Jack, whither may you be going?

Jack. Lord, Sir, to an hundred places at least. I shall be all over
the Town in less than half an Hour.

Codger. Nevertheless it is well known, you have no manner
of Business over any part of it. I am much afraid, Son Jack,
you will be a Blockhead all your life.

---

379 (*aside.*)] aside. *MS*

Lady Smatter. For shame, Mr. Codger! Jack, you were voted   400
into our Esprit Party last meeting; & if you come to night,
you will be admitted.

Jack. I'll come with the greatest pleasure, ma'am, if I can but
get away from Will. Scamper, but we are upon a frolic to
night, so it's ten to one if I can make off.

Mrs. Sapient. If I might take the liberty, Sir, to offer *my* advice upon this occasion, I should say that [10r] useful
friends were more improving than frivolous companions,
for, in *my* opinion, it is pity to waste Time.

Jack. Why, ma'am, that's just my way of thinking! I like to be   410
always getting forward, always doing something. Why I am
going now as far as Fleet Street, to a Print shop, where I left
Tom Whiffle. I met him in my way from Cornhill, &
promised to be back with him in half an Hour.

Beaufort. Cornhill? you said you were going to Hyde Park.

Jack. Yes, but I met Kit Filligree, & he hauled me into the
City. But, now you put me in mind of it, I believe I had best
run there first, & see who's waiting.

Beaufort. But what, in the mean Time, is to become of Tom
Whiffle?   420

Jack. O, hang him, he can wait.

Codger. In truth, Son Jack, you Scandalise me! I have even apprehensions for your Head; you appear to me to be *non
compos mentis*.

Beaufort. 'Tis pity, Jack, you cannot change situations with a
running Footman.

Jack. Ay, ay, good folks, I know you all love to cut me up, so
pray amuse yourselves your own way,— only don't expect
me to stay & hear you. (*going.*)

Codger. Son Jack, return. Pray answer me to the following   430
Question. [10v]

Jack. Dear Sir, pray be quick, for I'm in a horrid hurry.

---

401 last meeting] *ins*, last night *del*
412–415 Fleet Street and Cornhill are at opposite ends of the central City of
London. Hyde Park, in the residential suburb of Westminster, is some dis-
tance from both places, but is particularly far-removed from Cornhill.
420 Whiffle?] Whiffle. *MS*

Codger. A little more patience, Son, would become you better; you should consider that you are but a Boy, & that I am
your Father.

Jack. Yes, Sir, I do. Was that all, Sir?

Codger. All? why I have said nothing.

Jack. very true, Sir.

Codger. You ought, also, to keep it constantly in your Head
that I am not merely Older, but Wiser than yourself.   440

Jack. Yes, Sir. (*aside.*) Demme, though, if I believe that!

Codger. You would do well, also, to remember, that such
haste to quit my presence, looks as if you took no pleasure
in my Company.

Jack. It does so, Sir. (*aside.*) Plague take it, I sha'n't get away
this age.

Codger. Son Jack, I insist upon your minding what I say.

Jack. I will, Sir. (*going.*)

Codger. Why you are running away without hearing my
Question.   450

Jack. (*aside.*) O dem it, I shall never get off! [*to* **Codger.**]
Pray, Sir, what is it?

Codger. Don't Speak so quick, Jack, there's no understanding
a Word you say. one would think you supposed I was going
to take the trouble of asking a Question that was not of sufficient importance to deserve an answer.

Jack. True, Sir: but do pray be so good to make haste.

Codger. Son, once again, don't put yourself in such a fury;
[11r] you hurry me so, you have almost made me forget
what I wanted to ask you; let me see,— O, now I recollect;   460
pray do you know if the Fish was sent Home before you
came out?

Jack. Lord no, Sir, I know nothing of the matter! (*aside.*) How
plaguy tiresome! to keep me all this Time for such a Question as that.

Codger. Son Jack, you know nothing! I am concerned to say
it, but you know nothing!

Lady Smatter. Don't judge him hastily. Mr. Dabler, you seem
lost in thought.

---

451 (*aside.*)] aside. *MS*

Dabler. Do I, ma'am? I protest I did not know it.   470

Lady Smatter. O you are a sly Creature! Planning some
Poem, I dare Say.

Jack. I'll e'en take French leave.   *(going.)*

Cecilia. You are destined to be tormented this morning, *(following him.)* for I cannot suffer you to escape till we come
to an explanation: you said you had news for me?

Jack. O ay, true; I'll tell you what it was. While I was upon
'change this morning— but hold, I believe I'd best tell Lady
Smatter first.

Cecilia. Why So?   480

Jack. Because perhaps you'll be frightened.

Cecilia. Frightened? at what?

Jack. Why it's very bad news.

Cecilia. Good God, what can this mean?

Beaufort. Nothing, I dare be sworn. [11v]

Jack. Very well, Brother! I wish you may think it nothing
when you've heard it.

Cecilia. Don't keep me in suspence, I beseech you.

Beaufort. Jack, what is it you mean by alarming Miss Stanley
thus.   490

Jack. Plague take it, I wish I had not spoke at all! I shall have
him fly into another passion!

Cecilia. Why will you not explain yourself?

Jack. Why, ma'am, if you please, I'll call on you in the after-
noon.

Cecilia. No, no, you do but encrease my apprehensions by
this delay.

Beaufort. Upon my Honour, Jack, this is insufferable!

Jack. Why Lord, Brother, don't be so angry.

Lady Smatter. Nay, now Jack, you are really provoking.   500

---

473 French leave: "to depart without intimation, as in flight" (Eric Partridge,
ed., *A Dictionary of Slang and Unconventional English,* 7th ed. [New
York: MacMillan, 1970]).

478 'change: the Royal Exchange, a place in the city of London where mer-
chants gather to transact business. At this period, the main entrance of the
Exchange was on Cornhill street.

Mrs. Sapient. Why yes, I must needs own I am, myself, of opinion that it is rather disagreeable to wait long for bad news.

Codger. In truth, Jack, you are no better than a Booby.

Jack. Well, if you will have it, you will! but I tell you before hand you won't like it. You know Stipend, the Banker?

Cecilia. Good Heaven, know him? yes,— what of him?

Jack. Why— now, upon my Word, I'd rather not speak.

Cecilia. You sicken me with apprehension!

Jack. Well,— had you much money in his Hands?   510

Cecilia. Every thing I am worth in the World!

Jack. Had you faith?

Cecilia. You terrify me to Death!— what would you say?

Beaufort. No matter what,— Jack, I could murder you! [12r]

Jack. There, now, I said how it would be! now would not any body suppose the man broke through my fault?

Cecilia. Broke?— O Heaven, I am ruined!

Beaufort. No, my dearest Cecilia, your Safety is wrapt in mine, &, to my Heart's last sigh, they shall be inseparable.

Lady Smatter. Broke?— what can this mean?   520

Mrs. Sapient. Broke? who is broke? I am quite alarmed.

Codger. In truth, this has the appearance of a Serious Business.

Cecilia. Mr. Beaufort, let me pass— I can stand this no longer.

Beaufort. Allow me to conduct you to your own Room; this torrent will else over-power you. Jack, wait till I return.
                                        (*he leads* **Cecilia** *out.*)

Jack. No, no, Brother, you'll excuse me there!— I've stayed too long already.   (*going.*)

Lady Smatter. Hold, Jack. I have ten thousand Questions to ask you. Explain to me what all this means. It is of the utmost consequence I should know immediately.   530

Mrs. Sapient. I, too, am greatly terrified: I know not but I may be myself concerned in this transaction; & really the thought of losing one's money is extremely serious, for, as far as *I* have seen of the World, there's no living without it.

Codger. In truth, Son Jack, you have put us all into tribulation.

---

527 (*going.*)] going. *MS*

Mrs. Sapient. What, Sir, did you say was the Banker's
name? [12v]

Jack. (*aside.*) Lord, how they worry me! [*to **Lady Smatter.***]
Stipend, ma'am.

Mrs. Sapient. Stipend? I protest he has concerns with half   540
my acquaintance! Lady Smatter, I am in the utmost conster-
nation at this intelligence; I think one hears some bad news
or other every Day,— half the people one knows are ruined! I wish your Ladyship good morning. upon my word,
in *my* opinion, a Bankruptcy is no pleasant thing!

(Exit.)

Lady Smatter. Pray, Jack, satisfy me more clearly how this affair stands; tell me all you know of it?

Jack. (*aside.*) Lord, I sha'n't get away till midnight! [*to **Lady
Smatter.***] why ma'am, the man's broke, that's all.

Lady Smatter. But *how*? is there no prospect his affairs may   550
be made up?

Jack. None; they say upon 'Change there won't be a shilling
in the Pound.

Lady Smatter. What an unexpected blow! Poor Miss Stanley!

Dabler. 'Tis a shocking circumstance indeed. (*aside.*) I think
it will make a pretty good Elegy, though!

Lady Smatter. I can't think what the poor Girl will do! for
here is an End of our marrying her!

Dabler. 'Tis very hard upon her indeed. (*aside.*) 'Twill be the
most pathetic thing I ever wrote! [*to **Lady Smatter.***]   560
ma'am, your Ladyship's most obedient. [*aside.*] I'll to Work
while the subject is [13r] warm,— nobody will read it with
dry Eyes!   [*Exit.*]

---

538 (*aside.*)] aside. *MS*

543-544 half the people one knows are ruined: T.S. Ashton's *Economic Fluc-
tuations In England* (Oxford: The Clarendon Press, 1959) notes unusually
large numbers of bankruptcies in 1777-78 (162-3). *The Witlings* was written
in 1778-1779.

548 (*aside.*)] aside. *MS*

552 *Jack.*] Jack. *MS*

552-553 shilling in the Pound: the amount that may be recoverable from the
bankrupt estate.

561-563 [(*aside.*)] I'll ~ Eyes! [*exit.*]] I'll ~ Eyes! *aside & exit. MS*

Lady Smatter. I have the greatest regard in the World for
Miss Stanley,— nobody can esteem her more; but I can't
think of letting Beaufort marry without money.

Codger. Pray, madam, how came Miss Stanley to have such
very large concerns with Mr. Stipend?

Lady Smatter. Why he was not only her Banker, but her
Guardian, & her whole Fortune was in his Hands. She is a   570
pretty sort of Girl,— I am really grieved for her.

Jack. Lord, here's my Brother! I wish I could make off.

Re-enter Beaufort.

Beaufort. Stay, Sir! one word, & you will be most welcome to
go. Whence had you the intelligence you so humanely com-
municated to Miss Stanley?

Jack. I had it upon 'Change. Every body was talking of it.

Beaufort. Enough. I have no desire to detain you any longer.

Jack. Why now, Brother, perhaps you think I am not sorry for
Miss Stanley, because of my coming in such a hurry? but I
do assure you it was out of mere goodnature, for I made a   580
point of running all the way, for fear she should hear it
from a stranger.

Beaufort. I desire you will leave me: my mind is occupied
with other matters than attending to your defence.

Jack. Very well, Brother. Plague take it, I wish I had gone
[13v]to Hyde Park at once!   (*Exit.*)

Codger. In truth, Son Beaufort, I must confess Jack has been
somewhat abrupt; but, nevertheless, I must hint to you
that, when I am by, I think you might as well refer the due
reproof to be given by me. Jack is not every body's son, al-   590
though he be mine.

Beaufort. I am sorry I have offended you, Sir, but—

Codger. Madam, as your House seems in some little pertuba-
tion, I hope you will excuse the shortness of my visit if I
take leave now. Your Ladyship's most humble servant. Jack
is a good Lad at the bottom, although he be somewhat
wanting in solidity.   (*Exit.*)

---

569 *Lady Smatter.*] Lady Smatter. *MS*
572 *Jack.*] Jack. *MS*
585–586 gone / to Hyde] gone [*catchword* to] / Hyde

Beaufort. At length, thank Heaven, the House is cleared. O madam, will you not go to Miss Stanley? I have left her in an agony of mind which I had no ability to mitigate.   600

Lady Smatter. Poor thing! I am really in great pain for her.

Beaufort. Your Ladyship alone has power to soothe her,— a power which, I hope, you will instantly exert.

Lady Smatter. I will go to her presently— or send for her here.

Beaufort. Surely your Ladyship will go to *her*?— at such a Time as this, the smallest failure in respect—

Lady Smatter. As to that, Beaufort,— but I am thinking what the poor Girl had best do; I really don't know what to advise.   610

Beaufort. If I may be honoured with your powerful intercession, I hope to prevail with her to be mine immediately. [14r]

Lady Smatter. Pho, pho, don't talk so idly.

Beaufort. Madam!

Lady Smatter. Be quiet a few minutes, & let me consider what can be done.

Beaufort. But, while we are both absent, what may not the sweet Sufferer imagine?

Lady Smatter. Suppose we get her into the Country?— yet I know not what she can do when she is there; she can't   620 Live on Green Trees.

Beaufort. What does your Ladyship mean?

Lady Smatter. Nothing is so difficult as disposing of a poor Girl of Fashion.

Beaufort. Madam!

Lady Smatter. She has been brought up to nothing,— if she can make a Cap, 'tis as much as she can do,— &, in such a case, when a Girl is reduced to a Penny, what is to be done?

Beaufort. Good Heaven, madam, will Miss Stanley ever be reduced to a Penny, while I Live in affluence?   630

Lady Smatter. Beaufort,— to cut the matter short, you must give her up.

Beaufort. Give her up?

---

600 ability] *ins*, power *del*

Lady Smatter. Certainly; you can never suppose I shall consent to your marrying a Girl who has lost all her Fortune.
while the match seemed suitable to your expectations, & to
my intentions towards you, I readily countenanced it, but
now, it is quite a different thing,— all is changed, and—

Beaufort. No, madam, no, all is not changed, for the Heart of
Beaufort is unalterable! I loved Miss Stanley in [14v] pros-   640
perity,— in adversity, I adore her! I solicited her favour
when she was surrounded by my Rivals, & I will still suppli-
cate it, though she should be deserted by all the World besides. Her distress shall encrease my tenderness, her
poverty shall redouble my Respect, & her misfortunes shall
render her more dear to me than ever!

Lady Smatter. Beaufort, you offend me extremely. I have as
high notions of Sentiment & delicacy as you can have, for
the study of the fine arts, as Pope justly says, greatly en-
larges the mind; but, for all that, if you would still have me   650
regard you as a Son, you must pay me the obedience due to
a mother, & never suppose I adopted you to marry you to a
Beggar.

Beaufort. A Beggar?— Indignation Choaks me!— I must leave
you, madam,— the submission I pay you as a Nephew, &
the obedience I owe you as an adopted Son, will else both
give way to feelings I know not how to stifle!   (*Exit.*)
                    Lady Smatter alone.
This is really an unfortunate affair. I am quite distressed
how to act, for the Eyes of all the World will be upon me! I
will see the Girl, however, & give her a hint about Beau-   660
fort;— William!
                    Enter a Servant.
Tell Miss Stanley I beg to speak to her.   *Exit Servant.*
I protest I wish she was fairly out of the House! I never
cordially liked her,— she has not a grain of Taste, & her
Compliments are so cold, one has no pleasure in receiving

649-650 "the study . . . mind.": Pope did not write it, but Ovid (43 B.C.–A.D.
17 or 18) wrote ". . . a faithful study of the liberal arts humanizes character"
(*Ex Ponto*, The Loeb Classical Library, Trans., Arthur Leslie Wheeler [Cam-
bridge: Harvard University Press, 1939], 362–63).

[15r] them,— she is a most insipid thing! I sha'n't be sorry
to have done with her.

Enter Cecilia.

Miss Stanley, my dear, your Servant.

Cecilia. Oh madam!

Lady Smatter. Take courage; don't be so downcast,— a   670
noble mind, as I was reading the other Day, is always superior to misfortune.

Cecilia. Alas, madam, in the first moments of sorrow & disappointment, Philosophy & Rhetoric offer their aid in vain!
Affliction may, indeed, be alleviated, but it must first be
felt.

Lady Smatter. I did not expect, Miss Stanley, you would have
disputed this point with *me*; I thought, after so long studying matters of this sort, I might be allowed to be a better
Judge than a Young Person who has not studied them at all.   680

Cecilia. Good Heaven, madam, are you offended?

Lady Smatter. Whether I am or not, we'll not talk of it now;
it would be illiberal to take offence at a Person in distress.

Cecilia. Madam!

Lady Smatter. Do you think Jack may have been misin-
formed?

Cecilia. Alas no! I have just received this melancholy confir-
mation of his intelligence.   (*Gives Lady Smatter a Letter.*)

Lady Smatter. Upon my Word 'tis a sad thing! a sad stroke
upon my Word! however, you have good friends, & such   690
as, I dare say, will take care of you.

Cecilia. Take care of me, madam?

Lady Smatter. Yes, my dear, *I* will for one. And you should
[15v] consider how much harder such a Blow would have
been to many other poor Girls, who have not your resources.

Cecilia. My resources? I don't understand you?

Lady Smatter. Nay, my dear, I only mean to comfort you, &
to assure you of my continued regard; & if you can think of
any thing in which I can serve you, I am quite at your Com-   700
mand; nobody can wish you better. My House, too, shall always be open to you. I should scorn to desert you because

you are in distress. A mind, indeed, cultivated & informed,
as Shakespeare has it, will ever be above a mean action.

Cecilia. I am quite confounded!

Lady Smatter. In short, my dear, you will find *me* quite at
your disposal, & as much your Friend as in the sunshine of
your Prosperity:— but as to Beaufort—

Cecilia. Hold, madam! I now begin to understand your Lady-
ship perfectly.   710

Lady Smatter. Don't be hasty, my dear. I say as to Beaufort,
he is but a young man, & young men, you know, are mighty
apt to be rash; but when they have no independance, & are
of no profession, they should be very cautious how they dis-
oblige their Friends. Besides, it always happens that, when
they are drawn in to their own ruin, they involve—

Cecilia. No more, I beseech you, madam! I know not how
[16r] to brook such terms, or to endure such indignity. I
shall leave your Ladyship's House instantly, nor, while any
other will receive me, shall I re-enter it! Pardon me,   720
madam, but I am yet young in the school of adversity, & my
spirit is not yet tamed down to that abject submission to
unmerited mortifications which Time & long suffering can
alone render supportable.

Lady Smatter. You quite surprise me, my dear! I can't imagine what you mean. However, when your mind is more
composed, I beg you will follow me to my own Room. Till
then, I will leave you to your meditations, for, as Swift has
well said, 'tis vain to reason with a Person in a passion.

(Exit.)

Cecilia *alone.*

Follow you? no, no, I will converse with you no more.   730
cruel, unfeeling Woman! I will quit your inhospitable Roof,
I will seek shelter— alas where?— without fortune, destitute of Friends, ruined in circumstances, yet proud of
Heart,— where can the poor Cecilia seek shelter, peace or
protection? Oh Beaufort! 'tis thine alone to console me; thy

703–704 "A mind . . .action": no source discovered.

706 *Lady Smatter.*] Lady Smatter. *MS*

729 "'tis vain to reason with a person in a passion" : no source discovered.

sympathy shall soften my calamities, & thy fidelity shall instruct me to support them. Yet fly I must!— Insult ought
not to be borne, & those who twice risk, the third time deserve it.

End of Act the Second. [16v]

Act III.

Scene *a Dressing Room at Lady Smatter's.*
Enter **Lady Smatter**, *followed by* **Beaufort**.

Beaufort. Madam you distract me! 'tis impossible her intentions should be unknown to you,— tell me, I beseech you, whither she is gone? what are her designs? & why she deigned not to acquaint me with her resolution?

Lady Smatter. Why will you, Beaufort, eternally forget that it is the duty of every wise man, as Swift has admirably said, to keep his passions to himself?

Beaufort. She must have been *driven* to this Step,— it could never have occurred to her without provocation. Relieve me then, madam, from a suspence insupportable, & tell   10
me, at least, to what asylum she has flown?

Lady Smatter. Beaufort, you make me Blush for you!— Who would suppose that a Scholar, a man of cultivated talents, could behave so childishly? Do you remember what Pope has said upon this Subject?

Beaufort. This is past endurance!— no, madam, no!— at such a Time as this, his very name is disgustful to me.

Lady Smatter. How!— did I hear right?— the name of Pope disgustful?—

Beaufort. Yes, madam,— Pope, Swift, Shakespeare himself, &   20
every other name you can mention but that of Cecilia Stanley, is hateful to my Ear, & detestable to my remembrance.

Lady Smatter. I am thunderstruck!— this is downright blasphemy.

6-7 "duty . . . .himself": no source discovered
9 provocation. Relieve] ~, + *lc MS*
12 you!] ~ ? *MS*
14-15 "Pope . . . subject?": no quotation discovered

Beaufort. Good Heaven, madam, is this a Time to talk of Books & Authors?— however, if your Ladyship is cruelly [1r] determined to give me no satisfaction, I must endeavour to procure intelligence elsewhere.

Lady Smatter. I protest to you she went away without speaking to me; she sent for a Chair, & did not even let the Servants hear whither she ordered it.

Beaufort. Perhaps, then, she left a Letter for you?— O I am sure she did! her delicacy, her just sense of propriety would never suffer her to quit your Ladyship's House with an abruptness so unaccountable.

Lady Smatter. Well, well, whether she writ or not is nothing to the purpose; she has acted a very prudent part in going away, &, once again I repeat, you must give her up.

Beaufort. No, madam, never!— never while Life is lent me will I give up the tie that renders it most dear to me.

Lady Smatter. Well, Sir, I have only this to Say,— one must be given up, she or me,— the decision is in your own Hands.

Beaufort. Deign then, madam, to hear my final answer, & to hear it, if possible, with lenity. That your favour, upon every account, is valuable to me, there can be no occasion to assert, & I have endeavoured to prove my sense of the goodness you have so long shewn me, by all the gratitude I have been able to manifest: you have a claim undoubted to my utmost respect, & humblest deference; but there is yet another claim upon me,— a sacred, an irresistable claim,— Honour! And this were I to forego, not all your Ladyship's most unbounded liberality & munificence would prove adequate reparation for so dreadful, so attrocious a sacrifice!

(Enter Servant.)

Servant. Mr. Censor, my lady. [1v]

Lady Smatter. Beg him to walk up Stairs. I will put this affair into his Hands; *(aside.)* he is a sour, morose, ill-tempered Wretch, & will give Beaufort no Quarter.

(Enter Censor.)

Mr. Censor I am very glad to see you.

Censor. I thank your Ladyship. Where is Miss Stanley?

Lady Smatter. Why not at Home. O Mr. Censor, we have the

57 give] *cor, original word not legible*

saddest thing to tell you!— we are all in the greatest affliction,— poor Miss Stanley has met with the cruellist misfortune you can conceive.

Censor. I have heard the whole affair.

Lady Smatter. I am vastly glad you came, for I want to have a
little rational consultation with you. Alas, Mr. Censor, what
an unexpected stroke! You can't imagine how unhappy it
makes me.

Censor. Possibly not; for my Imagination is no reveller,— it
seldom deviates from the Bounds of probability.   70

Lady Smatter. Surely you don't doubt me?

Censor. No, madam, not in the least!

Lady Smatter. I am happy to hear you say so.

Censor. (*aside.*) You have but little reason if you understood
me. [(*to **Lady Smatter.***)] When does your Ladyship expect
Miss Stanley's return?

Lady Smatter. Why, really, I can't exactly say, for she left the
House in a sort of a hurry. I would fain have dissuaded her,
but all my Rhetoric was ineffectual,— Shakespeare himself
would have pleaded in vain! To say the truth, her Temper   80
is none of the most flexible; however, poor Thing, great al-
lowance ought to be made for her unhappy situation, for,
as the Poet has it, misfortune renders every body unamiable. [2r]

Censor. What Poet?

Lady Smatter. Bless me, don't you know? Well, I shall now
grow proud indeed if I can boast of making a Quotation
that is new to the learned Mr. Censor. My present Author,
Sir, is Swift.

Censor. Swift?— you have, then, some private Edition of his   90
Works?

Lady Smatter. Well, well, I won't be possitive as to Swift,—
perhaps it was Pope. 'Tis impracticable for any body that
reads so much as I do to be always exact as to an Author.
Why now, how many Volumes do you think I can run
through in one year's reading?

---

62 cruellist] *cor*, grav *or*

71 me?] ~ , MS

83–84 "Misfortune . . . unamiable": no source discovered.

Censor. More than would require 7 years to digest.

Lady Smatter. Pho, pho, but I study besides, & when I am preparing a Criticism, I sometimes give a whole Day to poring over only one Line. However, let us, for the present, quit these abstruse points, &, as Parnel says, "e'en talk a little like folks of this world." 100

Censor. Parnel?— you have, then, made a discovery with which you should oblige the Public, for that Line passes for Prior's.

Lady Smatter. Prior?— O, very true, so it is. Bless me, into what errors does extensive reading lead us! But to Business,— this poor Girl must, some way or other, be provided for, & my opinion is she had best return to her Friends in the Country. London is a dangerous place for Girls who have no Fortune. Suppose you go to her, & reason with her upon the subject? 110

Beaufort. You *do* know her Direction, then?

Lady Smatter. No matter; I will not have *you* go to her, whoever does. Would you believe it, Mr. Censor, this unthinking young man would actually marry the Girl without a Penny? However, it behoves me to prevent him, if only for example's Sake. That, indeed, is the chief motive which Governs me, for such [2v] is my *fatal pre-eminence*, as Addison calls

101 Thomas Parnell (1679-1718) was a contemporary and friend of Pope and Swift, best known for his poem, "A Night-Piece On Death," published posthumously in 1721.

101-102 "e'en . . . world."] "e'en talk a "little ~ world." In 1718, Matthew Prior (1664-1721) wrote the poem, "A Better Answer," from which this line comes. (*The Literary Works of Matthew Prior*, 2 vols. eds. H. Bunker Wright and Monroe Spears [Oxford: Clarendon Press, 1971], vol. 1: 450, line 4).

118 Although Addison's *Spectator* #101 (1711) concerns the burdens of eminent men, he never uses the phrase "fatal pre-eminence" (1: 422-426). In 1801-2, Burney used the character of Lady Smatter in another play called *The Woman Hater*, which, like *The Witlings*, was never performed; in that play, Smatter uses the phrase, *painful pre-eminence*, attributing it to Parnel. That phrase was used by Pope in his *Essay on Man* (1733-1734): "Painful preheminence! yourselves to view/ Above life's Weakness, and its comforts too." (*Poems*, vol. 3, pt. 1, 153, lines 267-268).

it, that, should I give way, my name will be quoted for a Licence to indiscreet marriages for Ages yet to come. 120

Censor. I hope, madam, the gratitude of the World will be adequate to the obligations it owes you.

Lady Smatter. Well, Mr. Censor, I will commit the affair to your management. This paper will tell you where Miss Stanley is to be met with, & pray tell the poor Thing she may always depend upon my protection, & that I feel for her most extremely; but, above all things, let her know she must think no more of Beaufort, for why should the poor Girl be fed with false hopes? It would be barbarous to trifle with her expectations. I declare I should hate myself were I 130 capable of such cruelty. Tell her so, Mr. Censor, & tell her—

Beaufort. Oh madam, forbear!— Heavens, what a Message for Miss Stanley! Dishonour not yourself by sending it. Is she not the same Miss Stanley who was so lately respected, carressed, & admired? whose esteem you sought? whose favour you solicited?— whose alliance you coveted?— Can a few moments have obliterated all remembrance of her merit? Shall *we* be treacherous, because *she* is unfortunate? must *we* lose our integrity, because *she* has lost her For- 140 tune? Oh madam, reflect, while it is yet Time, that the judgement of the World at large is always impartial, & let us not, by with-holding protection from Her, draw universal contempt & reproach upon Ourselves!

Lady Smatter. Beaufort, you offend me extremely. Do you suppose I have laboured so long at the fine arts, & studied so deeply the intricacies of Literature, to be taught, at last, the [3r] right rule of conduct by my Nephew? O Mr. Censor, how well has Shakespeare said rash & inconsiderate is youth!— but I must wave a further discussion of this point 150

---

137 solicited? *cor, ~ , or*
149-150 "Rash . . . youth.": Not from Shakespeare; a near parallel occurs in *De Senectute* (vi. 20) by Cicero (106-43 B.C.): "rashness is the product of the budding-time of youth, prudence of the harvest-time of age" (The Loeb Classical Library, Trans. William Armistead [Cambridge: Harvard University Press, 1959], 28-29).

at present, as I have some notes to prepare for our Esprit
Party of to night. But remember, Beaufort, that if you make
any attempt to see or Write to Miss Stanley, I will dis-own &
disinherit you. Mr. Censor, you will enforce this Doctrine,
& pray tell him, it was a maxim with Pope,— or Swift, I am
not sure which,— that resolution, in a cultivated mind, is
unchangeable.   (*Exit.*)

Beaufort & Censor.

Beaufort. By Heaven, Censor, with all your apathy & misanthropy, I had believed you incapable of listening to such in-
humanity without concern.   160

Censor. Know you not, Beaufort, that though we can all see
the Surface of a River, it's depth is only to be fathomed by
Experiment? Had my concern been shallow, it might have
babbled without impediment, but, as it was Strong & violent,
I restrained it, lest a torrent of indignation should have over-
flowed your future hopes, & laid waste my future influence.

Beaufort. Shew me, I beseech you, the Paper, that I may hasten to the lovely, injured Writer, & endeavour, by my fidelity & simpathy to make her forget my connections.

Censor. Not so fast, Beaufort. When a man has to deal with a   170
Lover, he must think a little of himself, for he may be sure
the Innamorato will think only of his Mistress.

Beaufort. Surely you do not mean to refuse me her Direction?[3v]

Censor. Indeed I do, unless you can instruct me how to sus-
tain the assault that will follow my surrendering it.

Beaufort. Why will you trifle with me thus? What, to you, is
the resentment of Lady Smatter?

Censor. How gloriously inconsistent is the conduct of a professed Lover! while to his Mistress he is all tame submission   180
& abject servility, to the rest of the World he is command-
ing, selfish & obstinate; every thing is to give way to him,
no convenience is to be consulted, no objections are to be
attended to in opposition to his wishes. It seems as if he
thought it the sole business of the rest of mankind to study

156-157 "Resolution . . . unchangeable": no source discovered.

his single Interest,— in order, perhaps, to recompence him
for pretending to his Mistress that he has no Will but hers.

Beaufort. Shew me the address,— then rail at your leisure.

Censor. You think nothing, then, of the disgrace I must incur
with this literary Phenomenon if I disregard her injunc-   190
tions? Will she not exclude me for-ever from the purlieus of
Parnassus?— Stun me with the names of Authors she has
never read?— & pester me with flimsy Sentences which
she has the assurance to call Quotations?—

Beaufort. Well, well, well!—

Censor. Will she not tell me that Pope brands a breach of
Trust as dishonourable?— that Shakespeare stigmatises the
meanness of Treachery?— And recollect having read in
Swift— that Fortitude is one of the cardinal virtues?—

Beaufort. Stuff & folly!— does it matter what she says?— the   200
Paper!— the Direction!—

Censor. Heavens, that a Woman whose utmost natural capacity will hardly enable her to understand the [4r] History of
Tom Thumb, & whose comprehensive faculties would be
absolutely baffled by the Lives of the 7 Champions of Christendom, should dare blaspheme the names of our noblest
Poets with Words that convey no ideas, & Sentences of
which the Sound listens in vain for the Sense!— O, she is
insufferable!

---

190 Phenomenon] *cor*, Phonomenon *or*

193 Sentences: maxims or aphorisms (*OED*).

203-206 In 1730, Henry Fielding (1707-54) used the popular chapbook tale,
Tom Thumb, as the basis of a play which parodied the heroic drama of the
day. An expanded version soon appeared under the title *The Tragedy of
Tragedies; or, The Life and Death of Tom Thumb the Great*. Although Fielding's play was popular, by the 1770s it was, according to *The London Stage*,
played only as a comic afterpiece. Censor's reference could be either to the
afterpiece or the chapbooks. *The Famous History of the Seven Champions
of Christendom*, a chivalric romance written about 1597 by Richard Johnson
(1573?-1659), relates the adventures of Saints George of England, Denis of
France, James of Spain, Anthony of Italy, Andrew of Scotland, Patrick of Ire-
land, and David of Wales, as they battle evil for the kingdom of God.

Beaufort. How unseasonable a discussion! yet you seem to   210
be more irritated at her folly about Books, than at her want
of feeling to the sweetest of her Sex.

Censor. True; but the reason is obvious,— Folly torments because it gives present disturbance,— as to want of feeling— 'tis a thing of Course. The moment I heard that Miss
Stanley had lost her Fortune, I was certain of all that would
follow.

Beaufort. Can you, then, see such treachery without rage or
emotion?

Censor. No, not without *emotion*, for base actions always ex-   220
cite contempt,— but *rage* must be stimulated by surprise:
no man is much moved by events that merely answer his
expectations.

Beaufort. Censor, will you give me the direction? I have niether Time nor patience for further uninteresting discussions. If you are determined to refuse it, say so; I have other
resources, & I have a Spirit resolute to essay them all.

Censor. It is no news to me, Beaufort, that a man may find
more ways than one to ruin himself; yet, whatever pleasure
may attend putting them in practice, I believe it seldom   230
happens when he is irreparably undone, that he piques
himself upon his Success.

Beaufort. I will trouble you no longer,— your Servant.

(*going.*) [4v]

Censor. Hold, Beaufort! Forget, for a few moments, the
Lover, & listen to me, not with passion but understanding.
Miss Stanley, you find, has now no dependence but upon
you;— you have none but upon Lady Smatter,— what follows?

Beaufort. Distraction, I believe,— I have nothing else before
me!   240

Censor. If, instantly & wildly, you oppose her in the first heat
of her determination, you will have served a Ten Years' ap-
prenticeship to her caprices, without any other payment
than the pleasure of having endured them. She will regard
your disobedience as rebellion to her Judgement, & resent
it with acrimony.

Beaufort. Oh misery of Dependance!— the heaviest toil, the

hardest labour, fatigue the most intense,— what are they
compared to the corroding servility of discontented Depen-
dance?   250

Censor. Nothing, I grant, is so painful to endure, but nothing
is so difficult to shake off; & therefore, as you are now situ-
ated, there is but one thing in the World can excuse your
seeking Miss Stanley.

Beaufort. Whatever it may be, I shall agree to it with trans-
port. Name it.

Censor. Insanity.

Beaufort. Censor, at such a Time as this, rallery is unpardonable.

Censor. Attend to me, then, in sober sadness. You must give   260
up all thoughts of quitting this House, till the ferocity of
your learned Aunt is abated.

Beaufort. Impossible!

Censor. Nay, prithee, Beaufort, act not as a Lunatic while you
disclaim Insanity. I will go to Miss Stanley [5r] myself, &
bring you an account of her situation.

Beaufort. Would you have me, then, submit to this Tyrant?

Censor. Would I have a Farmer, after sewing a Field, not wait
to reap the Harvest?

Beaufort. I will endeavour, then, to yield to your counsel;   270
but, remember Censor, my yielding is not merely reluc-
tant,— it must also be transitory; for if I do not speedily
find the good effects of my Self-denial, I will boldly & firmly
give up forever all hopes of precarious advantage, for the
certain, the greater, the nobler blessing of claiming my
lovely Cecilia,— though at the hazard of ruin & destruc-
tion!

Censor. And do you, Beaufort, remember in turn, that had I
believed you capable of a different conduct, I had never
ranked you as my Friend.   280

Beaufort. Oh Censor, how soothing to my anxiety is your
hard-earned, but most flattering approbation! Hasten, then,
to the sweet Sufferer,— tell her my Heart bleeds at her unmerited distresses,— tell her that, with her fugitive Self,
peace & Happiness both flew this mansion,— tell her that,
when we meet—

Censor. All these messages may be given!— but not till then, believe me! Do you suppose I can find no better topic for Conversation, than making Soft Speeches by proxy?

Beaufort. Tell her, at least, how much—   290

Censor. My good Friend, I am not ignorant that Lovers, Fops, fine Ladies & Chambermaids have all [5v] charters for talking nonsense; it is, therefore, a part of their business, & they deem it indispensable; but I never yet heard of any order of Men so unfortunate as to be under a necessity of listening to them   *Exit.*

Beaufort alone.

Dear, injured Cecilia! why cannot I be myself the Bearer of the faith I have plighted thee?— prostrate myself at thy feet, mitigate thy Sorrows, & share, or redress thy Wrongs! Even while I submit to captivity, I disdain the chains that bind   300 me,— but alas, I rattle them in vain! O happy Those who to their own industry owe their subsistence, & to their own fatigue & hardships their succeeding rest, & rewarding affluence! Now, indeed, do I feel the weight of Bondage, since it teaches me to envy even the toiling Husbandman, & laborious mechanic.

The Scene changes to an apartment at Mrs. Voluble's;
Dabler is discovered Writing.
Dabler.

The pensive maid, with saddest sorrow sad,— no, hang it, that won't do!— *saddest sad* will never do. With,— with— with *mildest,*— ay that's it!— *The pensive maid with mildest sorrow sad,*— I should like, now, to hear a man mend that line!— I shall [6r] never get another equal to it.— Let's see,— sad, bad, Lad, Dad,— curse it, there's never a Rhyme will do!— Where's the art of Poetry?— O, here,— now we shall have it; *(reads.)* Add,— hold, that will do at once,— *with mildest sorrow sad, shed Crystal Tears, & Sigh to Sigh did add.* Admirable! admirable by all   10 that's good! Now let's try the first Stanza, *(reads.)*

---

291 Lovers] Lo- | Lovers *MS*

7 the art of Poetry: In 1702, Edward Bysshe published *The Art of English Poetry*; one of its features is a Rhyming Dictionary.

Ye gentle Nymphs, whose Heart's are prone to love,
Ah, hear my Song, & ah! my Song approve;
And ye, ye glorious, mighty Sons of Fame,
Ye mighty Warriors—
How's this, two *mightys*?— hang it, that won't do!—
let's see,— ye *glorious* Warriors,— no, there's *glorious* before,— O curse it, now I've got it all to do over again!—
just as I thought I had finished it!— ye *fighting*,— no,— ye
towering, no;— ye,— ye— ye— I have it, by Apollo!   20
> *Enter* **Betty**.

Betty. Sir, here's a person below who—

Dabler, *starting up in a rage.* Now curse me if this is not too
much! What do you mean by interrupting me at my studies?
how often have I given orders not to be disturbed?

Betty. I'm sure, Sir, I thought there was no harm in just telling
you—

Dabler. Tell me nothing!— get out of the Room directly!— &
take care you never break in upon me again,— no, not if
the House be on Fire!— Go, I say!

Betty. Yes, Sir. [(*aside.*)] Lord, how masters & *Misisses* do   30
love scolding!   [***Exit.***][6v]
> **Dabler** *alone.*

What a provoking intrusion! just as I had Worked myself
into the true Spirit of Poetry!— I sha'n't recover my ideas
this half Hour. 'Tis a most barbarous thing that a man's retirement cannot be sacred. (*Sits down to write.*) Ye *fighting*,— no, that was not it,— ye— ye— ye— O curse it,
(*stamping.*) if I have not forgot all I was going to say! That
unfeeling, impenetrable Fool has lost me more ideas than
Would have made a fresh man's reputation. I'd rather have
given 100 Guineas than have seen her. I protest, I was   40
upon the point of making as good a Poem as any in the Language,— my numbers flowed,— my thoughts were
ready,— my Words glided,— but now, all is gone!— all
gone & evaporated! (*claps his Hand on his Forehead.*)

30-31 Yes, Sir. [(*aside.*)] ~ Scolding! [*Exit.*]] Yes, Sir. Lord ~ *aside, and
Exit. MS*
39 Would] *cor, original reading undecipherable.*

here's nothing left! nothing in the World!— What shall I do
to compose myself? Suppose I read?— why where the
Deuce are all the things gone? (*looking over his Papers.*)
O, here,— I wonder how my Epigram will read to Day,— I
think I'll shew it to Censor,— he has seen nothing like it of
late;— I'll pass it off for some Dead Poet's, or he'll never do   50
it justice;— let's see, suppose Pope?— no, it's too smart for
Pope,— Pope never wrote any thing like it!— well then,
suppose—

           *Enter **Mrs. Voluble**.*

O curse it, another interruption!

Mrs. Voluble. I hope, Sir, I don't disturb you?— I'm sure I
would not disturb you for the World, for I know nothing's
so troublesome; & I know you Gentlemen Writers dislike it
of all things; but I only just wanted to know if the Windows
were Shut, for fear of the Rain, for I asked Betty [7r] if she
had been in to see about them, but she said—   60

Dabler. They'll do very well,— pray leave them alone,— I am
extremely busy;— (*aside.*) I must leave these Lodgings, I
see!

Mrs. Voluble. O Sir, I would not stay upon any account, but
only sometimes there are such sudden showers, that if the
Windows are left open, half one's things may be spoilt, before one knows any thing of the matter. And if so much as a
paper of yours was to be damaged, I should never forgive
myself, for I'd rather all the Poets in the World should be
Burnt in one great Bon fire, than lose so much as the most   70
miniken bit of your Writing, though no bigger than my Nail.

Dabler. My dear Mrs. Voluble, you are very obliging.   (*aside.*)
She's a mighty good sort of Woman,— I've a great mind to
read her that Song:— no, this will be better. [(*to **Mrs. Voluble.***)] Mrs. Voluble, do you think you can keep a Secret?

Mrs. Voluble. O dear Sir, I'll defy any body to excell me in
that! I am more particular Scrupulous about Secrets than
any body.

Dabler. Well, then, I'll read you a little thing I've just been
composing, & you shall tell me your opinion of it.   80

---

72 *aside*] *ins*

(reads.) on a young lady blinded by Lightning.
>   Fair Cloris, now depriv'd of Sight,
> To Error ow'd her fate uneven;
>   Her Eyes were so refulgent bright
> The blundering Lightning thought them Heaven.
what do you think of it, Mrs. Voluble?

Mrs. Voluble. O, I think it the prettiest, most moving thing I ever heard in my life. [7v]

Dabler. Do you indeed?— pray sit down, Mrs. Voluble, I protest I never observed you were standing.   90

Mrs. Voluble. Dear Sir, you're vastly polite.   *(seats herself.)*

Dabler. So you really think it's pretty good, do you?

Mrs. Voluble. O dear yes, Sir; I never heard any thing I liked so well in my life. It's prodigious fine, indeed!

Dabler. Pray don't sit so near the Door, Mrs. Voluble; I'm afraid you will take Cold. *(aside.)* 'Tis amazing to me where this Woman picked up so much Taste!

Mrs. Voluble. But I hope, Sir, my being here is of no hindrance to you, because, if it is, I'm sure—

Dabler. No, Mrs. Voluble, *(looking at his Watch.)* I am   100
obliged to go out myself now. I leave my Room in your charge; let care be taken that no human Being enters it in my absence, & don't let one of my Papers be touched or moved upon any account.

Mrs. Voluble. Sir I shall lock the Door, & put the key in my Pocket. No body shall so much as know there's a paper in the House.   ***Exit Dabler.***

                     Mrs. Voluble *alone.*
    I believe it's almost a Week since I've had a good rummage of them myself. Let's see, is not this *'Sprit* Night? yes; & he won't come Home till very late, so I think I may as   110
well give them a fair look over at once.
                 (seats herself at the Table.)
Well, now, how nice & snug this is! What's here?
                     (takes up a Paper.)
                 Enter Bob.

Bob. Mother, here's Miss Jenny, the Milliner maker.

82 Cloris] *lc MS*

Mrs. Voluble. Is there? ask her to come up.

Bob. Lord, mother, why you would not have her come into Mr. Dabler's Room? why if he— [8r]

Mrs. Voluble. What's that to you? do you suppose I don't know what I'm about? you're never easy but when you're a talking,— always prate, prate, prate about something or other. Go & ask her to come up, I say.   120

Bob. Lord, one can't speak a Word!—   (*Exit.*)

Mrs. Voluble *alone.*

Have done, will you? mutter, mutter, mutter;— It will be a prodigious treat to Miss Jenny to come into this Room.

Enter Miss Jenny

Miss Jenny, how do do, my dear? this is very obliging of you. Do you know whose Room you are in?

Miss Jenny. No, ma'am.

Mrs. Voluble. Mr. Dabler's own Room, I assure you! And here's all his Papers; these are what he calls his *miniscrips.*

Miss Jenny. Well, what a heap of them!

Mrs. Voluble. And he's got 5 or 6 Boxes brimful besides.   130

Miss Jenny. Dear me! well, I could not do so much if I was to have the Indies!

Mrs. Voluble. Now if you'll promise not to tell a living Soul a Word of the matter, I'll read you some of them: but be sure, now, you don't tell.

Miss Jenny. Dear no, I would not for ever so much.

Mrs. Voluble. Well, then, let's see,— what's this? (*takes up a Paper.*) *Elegy on the Slaughter of a Lamb.*

Miss Jenny. O, pray let's have that.

Mrs. Voluble. I'll put it aside, & look out some more. *A Dialogue between a Tear & a Sigh,— verses on a young lady's fainting away—*   140

Miss Jenny. That must be pretty indeed! I dare say it will [8v] make us cry.

Mrs. Voluble. *An Epitaph on a Fly killed by a Spider; an—*

131-132 to have the Indies: references to the Indies "were used allusively for a region or a place yielding great wealth" (*OED*).
138 *Lamb.*] *Lamb,.* MS

*Enter **Bob**.*

Bob. Mother, here's a young Gentlewoman wants you.

Mrs. Voluble. A young Gentlewoman?— who can it be?

Bob. I never see her before. She's a deal smarter than Miss Jenny.

Miss Jenny. I'm sure I'd have come more Dressed, if I'd   150
known of seeing any body.

Mrs. Voluble. Well, I can't imagine who it is. I'm sure I'm
in a sad pickle. Ask her into the Parlour.

Miss. Jenny. Dear ma'am, you'd better by half see her here;
all the fine folks have their Company up Stairs, for I see a
deal of the Quality, by carrying Things Home.

Mrs. Voluble. Well then, ask her to come up.

Bob. But suppose Mr. Dabler—

Mrs. Voluble. Mind your own Business, Sir, & don't think to
teach me. Go & ask her up this minute.   160

Bob. I'm going, a'n't I?   (***Exit.***)

Mrs. Voluble. I do verily believe that Boy has no equal for
prating; I never saw the like of him,— his Tongue's always
a running.

*Re-enter **Bob**, followed by **Cecilia**.*

Bob. Mother, here's the young Gentlewoman.

Cecilia. I presume, ma'am, you are Mrs. Voluble?

Mrs. Voluble. Yes, ma'am.

Cecilia. I hope you will excuse this intrusion; & I must
beg the favour of a few minutes private Conversation with
you.   170

Mrs. Voluble. To be sure, ma'am. Bobby, get the lady a Chair.
I hope, ma'am, you'll excuse Bobby's coming in before
you; he's a sad rude Boy for manners. [9r]

Bob. Why the young Gentlewoman bid me herself; 'twas no
fault of mine.

Mrs. Voluble. Be quiet, will you? Jabber, jabber, jabber,—
there's no making you hold your Tongue a minute. Pray,
ma'am, do sit down.

Cecilia. I thank you, I had rather stand. I have but a few
Words to say to you, & will not detain you 5 minutes.   180

Miss Jenny. Suppose Master Bobby & I go down Stairs till the

lady has done? (*apart to* **Mrs. Voluble.**) Why Lord, Mrs.
Voluble, I know who that lady is as well as I know you!
why it's Miss Stanley, that we've been making such a heap
of things for.

Mrs. Voluble. Why you don't say so! what, the Bride?

Miss Jenny. Yes.

Mrs. Voluble. Well, I protest I thought I'd seen her some
where before. Ma'am, (*to Cecilia,*) I'm quite ashamed of
not recollecting you sooner, but I hope your goodness will   190
excuse it. I hope, ma'am, the good lady your Aunt is
well?— that is, your aunt that is to be?

Cecilia. If you mean Lady Smatter,— I believe she is well.—

Mrs. Voluble. I'm sure, ma'am, I've the greatest respect in
the World for her Ladyship, though I have not the pleasure
to know her; but I hear all about her from Mrs. Hobbins,—
to be sure, ma'am, you know Mrs. Hobbins, my Lady's
House-Keeper?

Cecilia. Certainly: it was by her Direction I came hither.

Mrs. Voluble. That was very obliging of her, I'm sure, & I   200
take your coming as a very particular favour. I hope,
ma'am, all the rest of the Family's well? And Mrs. Simper,
my lady's Woman? But I beg pardon for my ill manners,
ma'am, for to be sure, I ought first to have asked for Mr.
Beaufort. I hope he's well, ma'am?

Cecilia. I— I don't know— I believe,— I fancy he is.—

Mrs. Voluble. Well, he's a most agreeable Gentleman indeed,
ma'am, & I think—[9v]

Cecilia. If it is inconvenient for me to speak to you now—

Mrs. Voluble. Not at all, ma'am; Miss Jenny & Bobby can as   210
well divert themselves in the Parlour.

Miss Jenny. Dear me yes, I'll go directly.

Bob. And I'll go & sit in the Kitchen, & look at the clock, &
when it's 5 minutes, I'll tell Miss Jenny.

Miss Jenny. Come, then, Master Bobby. [*aside.*] She's very

215-217 Come . . . married. [(*Exit with Bob.*)]   ] Come ~ Bobby. She's
~ married. *aside, & Exit with Bob. MS*

melancholic, I think, for a young lady just going to be married. **[*Exit with Bob.*]**

Cecilia. The motive which has induced me to give you this trouble, Mrs. Voluble—

Mrs. Voluble. Dear ma'am, pray don't talk of trouble, for I'm   220
sure I think it none. I take it quite as a favour to receive a visit from such a young lady as you. But pray, ma'am, sit down; I'm quite ashamed to see you standing,— it's enough to tire you to Death.

Cecilia. It is not of the least consequence. A very unexpected & unhappy Event has obliged me, most
abrubtly, to quit the House of Lady Smatter, & if—

Mrs. Voluble. Dear ma'am, you surprise me! but I hope you have not parted upon account of any disagreement?

Cecilia. I must beg you to hear me. I have, at present, insu-   230
perable objections to visiting any of my Friends; & Mrs. Hobbins, who advised me to apply to you, said she believed you would be able to recommend me to some place where I can be properly accomodated till my affairs are settled.

Mrs. Voluble. To be sure, ma'am, I can. But pray, ma'am, may I make bold to ask the reason of your parting?

Cecilia. I am not, at present, at liberty to tell it. Do you recollect any place that— [10r]

Mrs. Voluble. O dear yes, ma'am, I know many. Let's see,—   240
there's one in King Street,— & there's one in Charles Street,— & there's another in— Lord, I dare say I know an Hundred! only I shall be very cautious of what I recommend, for it is not every place will do for such a lady as

---

241-242 According to Phillipa Glanville's *London In Maps* (London: The Connoisseur, 1972), there were at least five King Streets and three Charles Streets in London in the eighteenth century (120-121, 136-138, and 158-159). Frances Burney's sister, Esther, and her husband, Charles Rousseau Burney, lived on Charles St., Covent Garden, for a time (*Early Journals and Letters* 1: 139, n).

you. But pray, ma'am, where may Mr. Beaufort be? I hope
he has no Hand in this affair?

Cecilia. Pray ask me no Questions!

Mrs. Voluble. I'm sure, ma'am, I don't mean to be troublesome; & as to asking Questions, I make a point not to do it,
for I think that curiosity is the most impertinent thing in   250
the World. I suppose, ma'am, he knows of your being here?

Cecilia. No, no,— he knows nothing about me.

Mrs. Voluble. Well, that's quite surprising, upon my word!
To be sure, poor Gentleman, it must give him a deal of concern, that's but natural, & besides—

Cecilia. Can you name no place to me, Mrs. Voluble, that you
think will be eligible?

Mrs. Voluble. Yes sure, I can, ma'am. I know a lady in the
very next street, who has very genteel apartments, that will
come to about 5 or 6 Guineas a Week, for, to be sure, a   260
young lady of your Fortune would not chuse to give less.

Cecilia. Alas!

Mrs. Voluble. Dear ma'am, don't vex so; I dare say my lady
will think better of it; besides, it's for her Interest, for
though, to be sure, Mr. Beaufort will have a fine Income,
yet young Ladies of forty thousand Pounds Fortune a'n't to
be met with every Day; & the folks say, ma'am, that yours
will be full that. [10v]

Cecilia. I must entreat you, Mrs. Voluble, not to speak of my
affairs at present; my mind is greatly disordered, & I cannot   270
bear the Subject.

Mrs. Voluble. Dear ma'am, I won't say another word. To be
sure, nothing's so improper as talking of private affairs,—
it's a thing I never do, for really—

                 Enter Miss Jenny & Bob.

Miss Jenny. May we come in?

Mrs. Voluble. Lord no; why I ha'n't heard one single thing
yet.

Bob. It's a great deal past the 5 minutes. I've been looking at
the clock all the Time.

Miss Jenny. Well, then, shall we go again?   280

Cecilia. No, it is not necessary. Mrs. Voluble, you can be so

good as to answer my Question, without troubling any
body to leave the Room.

Miss Jenny. Then we'll keep at this side, & we sha'n't hear
what you say.   (*Miss Jenny* & **Bob** *walk aside.*)

Mrs. Voluble. What think you, ma'am, of that place I mentioned?

Cecilia. I mean to be quite private, & should wish for a situation less expensive.

Mrs. Voluble. Why sure, ma'am, you would not think of giv-   290
ing less than 5 Guineas a Week? That's just nothing out of
such a Fortune as yours.

Cecilia. Talk to me no more of my Fortune, I beseech you,—
I have none!— I have lost it all!—

Mrs. Voluble. Dear ma'am, why you put me quite in a cold
Sweat! lost all your Fortune?

Cecilia. I know not what I say!— I can talk no longer;— pray
excuse my incoherence;— & if you can allow me to remain
here for half an Hour, I may, in that [11r] Time perhaps
hear from my Friends, & know better how to guide myself.   300

Mrs. Voluble. Yes, sure, ma'am, I shall be quite proud of your
Company. But I hope, ma'am, you was not in earnest about
losing Fortune?

Cecilia. Let nothing I have said be mentioned, I beseech you;
converse with your Friends as if I was not here, & suffer me
to recover my composure in silence. (*Walks away.*)
(*aside.*) Oh Beaufort, my only hope & refuge! hasten to my
support, ere my Spirits wholly Sink under the pressure of
distressful Suspence.

Mrs. Voluble. Well, this is quite what I call a *nigma*! Miss   310
Jenny my dear, come here; I'll tell you how it is,— do you
know she's come away from Lady Smatter's?

Miss Jenny. Dear me!

Mrs. Voluble. Yes; & what's worse, she says she's lost all her
Fortune.

Miss Jenny. Lost all her Fortune? Lack a dasy! why then
whose to pay for all our things? why we've got such a heap
as will come to a matter of I don't know how much.

Mrs. Voluble. Well, to be sure it's a sad thing; but you're to

know I don't much believe it, for she said it in a sort of a   320
pet; & my notion is she has been falling out with her Sweat-
heart, & if so may be her Head's a little touched. Them
things often happens in the Quarrels of Lovers.

Enter Betty.

Betty. Ma'am here's a Gentleman wants the young lady.

Cecilia, *starting.* 'Tis surely Beaufort!— Beg him to walk up
Stairs.— Mrs. Voluble, will you excuse this liberty? [11v]

Mrs. Voluble. Yes, sure, ma'am.   (*Exit Betty.*)

Cecilia, *aside.* Dear, constant Beaufort!— how grateful to my
Heart is this generous alacrity!

Mrs. Voluble *aside to Miss Jenny.* I dare say this is her Sweet-   330
heart.

   Miss Jenny. Dear me, how nice! we shall hear all they say!

Enter Censor.

Cecilia. Mr. Censor!— good Heaven!

Censor. Miss Stanley I will not say I rejoice,— for, in truth, in
this place I grieve to see you.

Mrs. Voluble. Pray, sir, won't you sit down?

Censor. I thank you, madam, I had rather stand. Miss Stanley I
must beg the Honour of speaking to you alone.

Mrs. Voluble. O Sir, if you like it, I'm sure we'll go.

Censor. Ay, pray do.   340

Mrs. Voluble *aside to Miss Jenny.* This Gentleman is by no
means what I call a polite person. [(*to Censor.*)] Sir, I hope
you'll put the young lady in better Spirits; she has been
very low indeed since she came; &, Sir, if you should want
for any thing, I beg—

Censor. Do, good madam, be quick. I am in haste.

Mrs. Voluble. We're going directly, Sir. Come, Miss Jenny.
Bobby, you great oaf, what do you stand gaping there for?
why don't you go?

Bob. Why you would not have me go faster than I can, would   350
you?   (*Exit.*)

Mrs. Voluble. I would have you hold your Tongue, Mr. prate-
apace! always wrangling & wrangling. Come, Miss Jenny!

(*Exit.*)

Miss Jenny. I don't see why we might not as well have stayed
here.   (*Exit.*) [12r]

Cecilia & Censor.

Cecilia. By what means, sir, have you discovered me?— have you been at Lady Smatter's?— does any body there know where I am, except her Ladyship?

Censor. First let me ask you what possible allurement could draw you under this Roof? did you mean, by the volubility   360 of folly, to over-power the sadness of recollection? did you imagine that nonsense has the same oblivious quality as the Waters of Lethe? & flatter yourself that, by swallowing large Draughts, you should annihilate all remembrance of your misfortunes?

Cecilia. No, no! I came hither by the dire guidance of necessity. I wish to absent myself from my Friends till the real state of my affairs is better known to me. I have sent my Servant into the City, whence I expect speedy intelligence. Lady Smatter's Housekeeper assured me that the character   370 of this Woman was unblemished, & I was interested in no other enquiry. But tell me, I beseech you, whence you had your information of the calamity that has befallen me? & who directed you hither? & whether my Letter has been shewn or concealed?— & what I am to infer from *your* being the first to seek me?

Censor. Pray go on!

Cecilia. Sir!

Censor. Nay, if you ask 40 more Questions without waiting for an answer, I have messages that will more than keep pace   380 with your enquiries; therefore ask on, & spare not! [12v]

Cecilia, disconcerted. No, Sir, I have done!

Censor. How! have I, then, discovered the art of silencing a Lover? Hasten to me, ye wearied Guardians of pining youth, I will tell ye a Secret precious to ye as repose! fly hither, ye sad & solemn Confidents of the love-lorn tribe, for I can point out relief to exhausted Patience!

Cecilia. Spare this rallery, I beseech you;— & keep me not in suspence as to the motive of your visit.

Censor. My first motive is the desire of seeing,— my second   390 of serving you; if indeed, the ill-usage you have experienced from one Banker, will not intimidate you from trusting in another.

Cecilia. How am I to understand you?

Censor. As an honest man! or, in other Words, as a man to whose Friendship distressed Innocence has a claim indisputable.

Cecilia. You amaze me!

Censor. It must be some Time ere your affairs can be settled, & the loss of Wealth will speedily, & roughly make you know it's value. Consider me, therefore, as your Banker, & draw upon me without reserve. Your present situation will teach you many Lessons you are ill prepared to learn; but Experience is an unfeeling master, whose severity is niether to be baffled by youth, nor softened by Innocence. Suppose we open our account to Day?— this may serve for a beginning; (*presenting a Paper.*) I will call again to-morrow for fresh orders. (*going.*) 400

Cecilia. Stay, stay Mr. Censor!— amazement has, indeed, [13r] silenced me, but it must not make me forget myself. Take back, I entreat you, this paper— 410

Censor. Probably you suspect my motives? &, if you do, I am the last man whom your doubts will offend; they are authorised by the baseness of mankind, &, in fact, suspicion, in Worldly transactions, is but another Word for common sense.

Cecilia. Is it, then, possible you can think so ill of all others, & yet be so generous, so benevolent yourself?

Censor. Will any man follow an Example he abhors to look at? Will you, for instance, because you see most Women less handsome than yourself, ape deformity in order to resemble them? 420

Cecilia. O how little are you known, & how unjustly are you judged! For my own part, I even regarded you as my Enemy, & imagined that, if you thought of me at all, it was with ill-will.

Censor. In truth, madam, my character will rather encrease than diminish your surprise as you become more acquainted with it. you will, indeed, find me an odd fellow; a fellow who can wish you well without loving you, &, with- 430

___
413 doubts] *ins*, suspicions *del*

out any sinister view, be active in your Service; a fellow, in
short, unmoved by Beauty, yet susceptible of pity,— invul-
nerable to Love, yet zealous in the cause of distress. If you
accept my good offices, I shall ever after be your Debtor for
the esteem your acceptance will manifest,— if you reject
them, I shall but conclude you have the same [13v] indig-
nant apprehensions of the depravity of your fellow Creatures that I harbour in my own Breast.

Cecilia. If, hitherto I have escaped misanthropy, think you,   440
Sir, an action such as this will teach it me? no; I am
charmed with your generous offer, & shall henceforward
know better how to value you; but I must beg you to take
back this paper, (*returns it.*) I have at present no occasion
for assistance, & I hope— but tell me, for uncertainty is torture, have you, or have you not been at Lady Smatter's?

Censor. I have; & I come hither loaded with as many messages as ever abigail was charged with for the milliner of a
fantastic Bride. The little Sense, however, comprised in
their many Words, is briefly this; Lady Smatter offers you   450
her protection,— which is commonly the first Step towards
the insolence of avowed superiority: & Beaufort—

Cecilia. Beaufort?— Good Heaven!— did Mr. Beaufort know
whither you were coming?

Censor. He did; & charged with as many vows, supplications,
promises, & tender nonsences, as if he took my memory for
some empty habitation that his Fancy might furnish at it's
pleasure. He Commissioned me—

Cecilia. Oh Heaven! (*weeps.*)

Censor. Why how now? he commissioned me, I say—

Cecilia. Oh faithless Beaufort! lost, lost Cecilia!   460

Censor. To sue for him,— Kneel for him,—

Cecilia. Leave me, leave me, Mr. Censor!— I can hear no
more. [14r]

Censor. Nay, pritheee, madam, listen to his message.

Cecilia. No, Sir, never! at such a Time as this, a message is an
Insult! He must know I was easily to be found, or he would
not have sent it, &, knowing that, whose was it to have

---

447 abigail: Generic name for a maid or waiting-woman, probably derived
from the Abigail of *1 Samuel* (*OED*).

sought me?— Go, go, hasten to your Friend,— tell him I
heard all that it became me to hear, & that I understood
him too well to hear more: tell him that I will save both   470
him & myself the disgrace of a further explanation,— tell
him, in short, that I renounce him for ever!

Censor. Faith, madam, this is all beyond my comprehension.

Cecilia. To desert me at such a Time as this! to know my
abode, yet fail to seek it! to suffer my wounded Heart,
bleeding in all the anguish of recent calamity, to doubt his
Faith, & suspect his tenderness!

Censor. I am so totally unacquainted with the Laws & maxims
necessary to be observed by fine Ladies, that it would ill become me to prescribe the limits to which their use of rea-   480
son ought to be contracted; I can only—

Cecilia. Once more, Mr. Censor, I must beg you to leave
me. Pardon my impatience, but I cannot converse at present. Ere long, perhaps, indignation may teach me to suppress my Sorrow, & Time & Reason may restore my tranquility.

Censor. Time, indeed, may possibly stand your Friend, [14v]
because Time will be regardless of your impetuosity, but
Faith, madam, I know not what right you have to expect
Succor from Reason, if you are determined not to hear it.   490
Beaufort, I say—

Cecilia. Why will you thus persecute me? nothing can extenu-
ate the coldness, the neglect, the insensibility of his conduct. Tell him that it admits no palliation, & that hence-
forth— no, tell him nothing,— I will send him no
message,— I will receive none from him,— I will tear his
Image from my Heart,— I will forget, if possible, that there
I cherished it!—

Enter Mrs. Voluble.

Mrs. Voluble. I hope I don't disturb you, Sir? Pray, ma'am,
don't let me be any hindrance to you; I only just come to   500
ask if you would not have a bit of Fire, for I think it's grown
quite cold. What say you, Sir? pray make free if you like it.
I'm sure I would have had one before if I had known of
having such company; but really the Weather's so change-

able at this Time of the year, that there's no knowing what
to do. Why this morning I declare it was quite hot. We
Breakfasted with both the Windows open. As to Bobby, I
verily thought he'd have caught his Death, for he would
not so much as put his Coat on.

Censor. Intolerable! the man who could stand this, would   510
Sing in the Stocks, & Laugh in the Pillory!— Will you, Miss
Stanley, allow me 5 minutes conversation to explain—
[15r]

Mrs. Voluble. I beg that my being here may not be any stop
to you, for I'll go directly if I'm in the way. I've no notion
of prying into other people's affairs,— indeed, I quite make
it a rule not to do it, for I'm sure I've business enough of
my own, without minding other Peoples. Why now, Sir,
how many things do you think I've got to do before night?
Why I've got to—   520

Censor. O pray, good madam, don't make your complaints to
me,— I am hard of Heart, & shall be apt to hear them without the least compassion. Miss Stanley—

Mrs. Voluble. Nay, Sir, I was only going—

Censor. Do prithee, good Woman, give me leave to speak.
Miss Stanley, I say—

Mrs. Voluble. Good Woman! I assure you, Sir, I'm not used to
be spoke to in such a way as that.

Censor. If I have called you by an apellation opposite to your
character, I beg your pardon; but—   530

Mrs. Voluble. I can tell you, Sir, whatever you may think of it,
I was never called so before; besides,—

Censor. Miss Stanley, some other Time—

Mrs. Voluble. Besides, Sir, I say, I think in one's own House
it's very hard if—

Censor. Intolerable! Surely this Woman was sent to satirize
the use of Speech! once more—

Mrs. Voluble. I say, Sir, I think it's very hard if—

Censor. Miss Stanley, your most obedient!   (*Exit abruptly.*)

Mrs. Voluble. Well, I must needs say, I think this is [15v] the   540

---

518 minding] *cor,* prying *or*

rudest fine Gentleman among all my acquaintance. Good
Woman, indeed! I wonder what he could see in me to
make use of such a Word as that! I won't so much as go
down Stairs to open the Street Door for him,— yes I will,
too, for I want to ask him about—   (*Exit talking.*)

Cecilia *alone.*

Hast thou not, Fortune, exhausted, now, thy utmost
severity?— reduced to Poverty,— abandoned by the
World,— betrayed by Beaufort,— what more can I fear?—
Beaufort, on whose constancy I relied,— Beaufort, from
whose simpathy I expected consolation,— Beaufort, on   550
whose Honour, delicacy & Worth I founded Hopes of
sweetest tranquility, of lasting happiness, of affection unalterable! Oh hopes for-ever blighted! Oh Expectations eternally destroyed! Oh fair & lovely tranquility— thou hast
flown this Bosom, never, never more to revisit it!

Re-enter *Mrs. Voluble*

Mrs. Voluble. I could not overtake him all that ever I could
do, & yet I went as fast as— Lord, ma'am, sure you a'n't a
crying?

Cecilia. Loss of Fortune I could have borne with patience,—
change of situation I could have suffered with fortitude,—   560
but such a Stroke as this!— [16r]

Mrs. Voluble. Poor young lady!— I declare I don't know
what to think of to entertain her.

Cecilia. Oh Beaufort! had our situations been reversed, would
such have been my conduct?

Mrs. Voluble. Come, dear ma'am, what signifies all this fretting? If you'll take my advice—

Enter *Betty.*

Betty. Do pray, ma'am, Speak to master Bobby,— he's a turning the House out of Windows, as a body may say.

Mrs. Voluble. Well, if I don't believe that Boy will be the   570
Death of me at last!— only think, ma'am, what a plague he

568–569 turning the House out of Windows: "to make a great noise or disturbance in a house" (Partridge, *Dictionary of Slang*).

is to me! I'm sure I have my misfortunes as well as other
people, so you see, ma'am, you a'n't the only person in
trouble.— Why ma'am, I say!— did not you hear Betty?—
She Says that Bobby—

Cecilia. O for a little repose!— leave me to myself, I beseech
you! I can niether speak or listen to you;— pray go,—
pray— alas, I know not what I say!— I forget that this
House is yours, & that I have no right even to the shelter
it's Roof affords me.   580

Mrs. Voluble. Dear ma'am, pray take a little comfort,—

Cecilia. Have you, madam, any Room which for a few Hours
you can allow me to call my own?— where, unmolested &
alone, I may endeavour to calm my mind, & settle some
plan for my future conduct? [16v]

Mrs. Voluble. Why, ma'am, the Room over-head is just such
another as this, & if it's agreeable—

Cecilia. Pray shew it me,— I'm sure it will do.

Mrs. Voluble. I only wish, ma'am, it was better for your sake;
however, I'll make it as comfortable as ever I can, & as   590
soon—   *Exit, talking, with Cecilia*
                        Betty alone.

I'll be Hanged, now, if it is not enough to provoke a
Stork to live in such a House as this! one may clean & clean
for-ever, & things look never the better for it. As to Master
Bobby, he does more mischief than his Head's worth; & as
to my *Mississ*, if she can but keep talk, talk, talk, she don't
care a pin's point for nothing else.
                Re-enter Mrs. Voluble.

Why Betty, what do you stand there for?— Do you think
I keep you to look at?

Betty. you won't keep me for nothing long.   (*Exit Betty.*)   600
                Mrs. Voluble alone.

There, now, that's the way with all of them! if one does
but say the least thing in the World, they're ready to give
one Warning. I declare Servants are the plague of one's
Lives. I've got a good mind to— Lord, I've got so many
things to do, I don't know what to set about first! Let me
see, (*seats herself.*) now I'll count them over. In the first

place, I must see after a Porter to [17r] carry the lady's message;— then I must get the best Plates ready against Mrs.
Wheedle comes;— after that, I must put Mr. Dabler's pa-
pers in order, for fear of a Surprise;— then I must get in a   610
little bit of something nice for Supper;— then— Oh Lord, if
I had not forgot that *'scape Grace* Bobby!

(*runs off.*)

End of Act the Third . [17v]

Act IV.

A Library at Lady Smatter's.
Lady Smatter, Mrs. Sapient, Dabler and Codger,
Seated at a round Table covered with Books.

Lady Smatter. Now before we begin our Literary Subjects, allow me to remind you of the rule established at our last meeting, That every one is to speak his real sentiments, & no flattery is to taint our discussions.

All. Agreed.

Lady Smatter. This is the smallest assembly we have had yet; some or other of our members fail us every Time.

Dabler. But where such luminaries are seen as Lady Smatter & Mrs. Sapient, all other could only appear to be Eclipsed.

Lady Smatter. What have you brought to regale us with to night, Mr. Dabler?   10

Dabler. Me? dear ma'am, nothing!

Lady Smatter. Oh barbarous!

Mrs. Sapient. Surely you cannot have been so cruel? for, in *my* opinion, to give pain causelessly is rather disobliging.

Dabler. Dear Ladies, you know you may command me; but, I protest, I don't think I have any thing worth your hearing. [1r]

Lady Smatter. Let us judge for ourselves. Bless me, Mr. Codger, how insensible you are! why do you not join in our   20
entreaties?

Codger. For what, madam?

Lady Smatter. For a Poem, to be sure.

Codger. Madam, I understood Mr. Dabler he had nothing worth your hearing.

Lady Smatter. But surely you did not believe him?

Codger. I knew no reason, madam, to doubt him.

Lady Smatter. O you Goth! come, dear Mr. Dabler, produce something at once, if only to shame him.

---

28 Goth: i.e., barbarian (*OED*).

Dabler. Your Ladyship has but to Speak.   30
          (Takes a Paper from his Pocket Book, & reads.)
               on a certain *Party* of Beaux Esprits.
     Learning, here, doth pitch her Tent,
          Science, here, her Seeds doth Scatter;
     Learning, in form of Sapient,
          Science, in guise of heav'nly Smatter.
Lady Smatter. O charming! beautiful Lines indeed.
Mrs. Sapient. Elegant & poignant to a degree!
Lady Smatter. What do *you* think, Mr. Codger, of this Poem?
     to be sure, *(whispering him.)* the compliment to Mrs. Sapi-
     ent is preposterously overstrained, but, otherwise, nothing   40
     can be more perfect. [1v]
Mrs. Sapient. Mr. Dabler has, indeed, the happiest turn in
     the World at easy elegance. Why, Mr. Codger, you don't
     speak a Word? Pray, between friends, *(whispering him.)*
     what say you to the notion of making Lady Smatter repre-
     sent Science? don't you think he has been rather unskillful
     in his choice?
Codger. Why, madam, you give me no Time to think at all.
Lady Smatter. Well, now to other matters. I have a little ob-
     servation to offer upon a Line of Pope; he says   50
          Most Women have no Character at all;
     Now I should be glad to know, if this was true in the Time
     of Pope, why People should complain so much of the de-
     pravity of the present age?
Dabler. Your Ladyship has asked a Question that might per-
     plex a Solomon.
Mrs. Sapient. It is, indeed, surprisingly ingenious.
Dabler. Yes, & it reminds me of a little foolish thing which I
     composed some Time ago.
Lady Smatter. O pray let us hear it.   60

---

31 *Party*] the underlining, in pencil, is a later addition to the MS
34 Science: Any body of organized knowledge (*OED*).
44 *(whispering him.)*] *cor, whispering him or*
51 "Most Women . . . ." : From Pope's *Moral Essays* (1731–1735), the quotation is the second line of Epistle II: "To a Lady: Argument of the Characters
of Women" (*Poems*, vol. 3, part 2, 45). Lady Smatter, correct in this instance,
has obviously prepared in advance.

Dabler. Your Ladyship's commands—
     The lovely Iris, young & fair,
     Possess'd each charm of Face & air
     That with the Cyprian might compare; [2r]
     So sweet her Face, so soft her mind,
     So mild she speaks,— she looks so kind,—
     To hear— might melt!— to see,— might blind!

Lady Smatter. .   .   . O elegant! enchanting! delicious!
           together
Mrs. Sapient. .   .   . O delightful! pathetic! delicate!

Lady Smatter. Why Mr. Codger, have you no Soul? is it possi-   70
ble you can be unmoved by such poetry as this?

Codger. I was considering, madam, what might be the allu-
sion to which Mr. Dabler referred, when he said he was re-
minded of this little foolish thing, as he was pleased to call
it himself.

Dabler. <(*aside.*) I should like to toss that old fellow in a
Blanket!>

Codger. Now, Sir, be so good as to gratify me by relating
what may be the connection between your Song, & the
fore-going Conversation?   80

Dabler. *Pettishly.* Sir, I only meant to read it to the Ladies.

Lady Smatter. I'm sure you did us great honour. Mrs. Sapient, the next proposition is yours.

Mrs. Sapient. Pray did your Ladyship ever read Dryden?

Lady Smatter. Dryden? O yes!— but I don't just now recollect him;— let's see, what has he writ?

Dabler. Cymon & Iphigenia. [2v]

Lady Smatter. O ay, so he did; & really for the Time of Day I
think it's mighty pretty.

Dabler. Why yes, it's well enough; but it would not do now.   90

---

64 Cyprian: stock name for Venus, who is associated with the island of Cyprus.
68-69 **Lady Smatter** . . . **Lady Smatter.** . . .
          together]   *together*
     Mrs. Sapient . . . **Mrs. Sapient** . . .
76-77 marked for possible excision in MS
87 *Cymon & Iphigenia*: part of *Fables Ancient and Modern* (1700), published by John Dryden (1631-1700). The story of Cymon and Iphegenia was
not written by Dryden, but was translated by him from a poem by Boccacio.

Mrs. Sapient. Pray what does your Ladyship think of the
Spectator?

Lady Smatter. O, I like it vastly. I've just read it.

Codger, *to Lady Smatter.* In regard, madam, to those Verses
of Mr. Dabler, the chief fault I have to find with them, is—

Dabler. Why, Sir, we are upon another Subject now!
<(*aside.*) What an old Curmudgeon! he has been pondering
all this Time only to find fault!>

Mrs. Sapient. For *my* part, I have always thought that the
best papers in the Spectator are those of Addison.   100

Lady Smatter. Very justly observed!

Dabler. Charmingly said! exactly my own opinion.

Mrs. Sapient. Nay, I may be mistaken; I only offer it as my
private Sentiment.

Dabler. I can but wish, Madam, that poor Addison had Lived
to hear such praise.

Lady Smatter. Next to Mr. Dabler, my favourite Poets are
Pope & Swift.

Mrs. Sapient. Well, after all, I must confess I think there
are as many pretty things in old Shakespeare as in any   110
body.

Lady Smatter. Yes, but he is too common; *every* body can
speak well of Shakespeare!

Dabler. I vow I am quite sick of his Name.

Codger. Madam, to the best of my apprehension, I conceive
your Ladyship hath totally mistaken that Line of Pope
which says

    Most Women have no Character at all.[3r]

Lady Smatter. Mistaken? how so, sir? This is curious enough!
<(*aside to Dabler.*) I begin to think the poor Creature is   120
Superannuated.>

---

92 *The Spectator*: a collection of essays primarily by Joseph Addison and Sir
Richard Steele; it was published as a periodical in the years 1711-1712,
1714, and issued in book form soon afterward.

97-98 (*aside.*) . . . fault!] marked for possible excision in MS

99-100 I have always thought . . . . Addison: Mrs. Sapient's literary cliches
are similar to those of Samuel Johnson's Dick Minim in *The Idler*
(1758-1760), numbers 60-61.

120-121 marked for possible excision in MS

Dabler. So do I, ma'am; I have observed it for some Time.

Codger. By *no* Character, madam, he only means—

Lady Smatter. A *bad* Character, to be sure!

Codger. There, madam, lieth your Ladyship's mistake; he means, I say—

Lady Smatter. O dear Sir, don't trouble yourself to tell *me* his meaning;— I dare say I shall be able to make it out.

Mrs. Sapient aside to Dabler. How irritable is her Temper!

Dabler. O, intolerably!   130

Codger. Your Ladyship, madam, will not hear me. I was going—

Lady Smatter. If you please, Sir, we'll drop the subject, for I rather fancy you will give me no very new information concerning it,— do you think he will, Mr. Dabler?

Codger. Mr. Dabler, Madam, is not a competent Judge of the case, as—

Dabler, rising. Not a Judge, Sir? not a Judge of Poetry?

Codger. Not in the present circumstance, Sir, because, as I was going to Say—   140

Dabler. Nay then, Sir, I'm sure I'm a Judge of nothing!

Codger. That may be, Sir, but is not to the present purpose; [3v] I was going—

Dabler. Suppose, Sir, we refer to the Ladies? Pray, now, Ladies, which do *you* think the most adequate Judge of Poetry, Mr. Codger, or your humble Servant? Speak sincerely, for I hate flattery.

Mrs. Sapient. I would by no means be so ill bred as to determine for Mr. Dabler in the presence of Mr. Codger, because *I* have always thought that a preference of one person implies less approbation of another; yet—   150

Codger. Pray, madam, let me speak; the reason, I say—

Mrs. Sapient. Yet the well-known skill of Mr. Dabler in this delightful art—

Codger. Madam, this interruption is somewhat injudicious, since it prevents my explaining—

Mrs. Sapient rising. Injudicious, Sir? I am sorry, indeed, if I have merited such an accusation: there is nothing I have more scrupulously endeavoured to avoid, for, in *my* opin-

ion, to be injudicious is no mark of an extraordinary under-   160
standing.

Lady Smatter *aside to Dabler.* How soon she's hurt!

Dabler. O most unreasonably!

Codger. Madam you will never hear me out; you prevent my
explaining the reason, I say, why Mr. Dabler cannot decide
upon Lady Smatter's error in judgement—

Lady Smatter, *rising.* Error in judgement? really this is very
diverting! [4r]

Codger. I say, madam—

Lady Smatter. Nay, Sir, 'tis no great matter; & yet, I must   170
confess, it's rather a hard case that, after so many years of
intense Study, & most laborious reading, I am not allowed
to criticise a silly line of Pope.

Dabler. And if I, who, from infancy have devoted all my Time
to the practice of Poetry, am now thought to know nothing
of the matter,— I should be glad to be informed who has a
better Title?

Mrs. Sapient. And if I, who, during my whole life, have made
propriety my peculiar Study, am now found to be deficient
in it,— I must really take the liberty to observe that I must   180
have thrown away a great deal of Time to very little purpose.

Lady Smatter. And as to this line of Pope—
Enter a Servant.

Servant. Mr. Censor, my lady, begs to speak to your Ladyship
for only 2 minutes upon Business of consequence.

Dabler. Censor? Suppose we admit him?— (*aside.*) 'twill be
an admirable opportunity to shew him my Epigram.

Lady Smatter. Admit him? what, to ask his opinion of Mr.
Codger's critical annotations?

Codger. My doubt, madam, is, if you will give him Time to   190
speak it.

Lady Smatter. Well, is it agreeable to ye all that Mr. Censor
[4v] should have admittance? I know it is contrary to rule,

---

174 I, who from ~] I, who <almost *del*> from ~

174 Time] *ins*, thoughts *del*

183 . . . line of Pope—: a number of xx's are pencilled between this line and
the following stage direction. Their purpose is unclear.

yet, as he is one of the Wits, & therefore ought to be among us, suppose we indulge him?

Codger. Madam I vote against it.

Dabler aside to Lady Smatter. I see he's afraid of him,— let's have him by all means.

Lady Smatter. Without doubt. Pray, Mr. Codger, why are you against it?   200

Codger. Because, madam, there are already so many talkers that I cannot be heard myself.

Dabler. (*aside to Lady Smatter.*) You see how it is?

Lady Smatter. Yes, & enjoy it of all things. Desire Mr. Censor to Walk up stairs. (*Exit Servant.*) To be sure this is rather a deviation from the maxims of the society, but great minds, as a favourite author of mine observes, are above being governed by common prejudices.

Codger. I am thinking, madam,—

Enter Censor.

<*Lady Smatter.* Mr. Censor, your Entrance is most critically   210
fortunate; give me leave to present you to our society.>

<*Censor.* I expected to have seen your Ladyship alone.>

<*Lady Smatter.* Yes, but I have obtained a dispensation for your admittance to our Esprit Party. But let us not waste our Time in common conversation. You must know we are at present discussing a very knotty point, & I [5r] should be glad of your opinion upon the merits of the cause.>

<*Dabler.* Yes; & as soon as that is decided, I have a little choice piece of Literature to communicate to you which I think you will allow to be tolerable.>   220

<*Mrs. Sapient.* And I, too, Sir, must take the liberty to appeal to your Judgement concerning—>

<*Censor.* Ay, ay, Speak all at a Time, & then one hearing may do.>

<*Lady Smatter.* Mr. Censor, when a point of the last importance is in agitation, such levity as this—->

Censor. Why, madam, the Business which brings me hither.

Dabler. Business? o name not the Word in this Region of Fancy & Felicity.

210–226 Bracketed in MS as though for future excision.

Mrs. Sapient. That's finely said, Mr. Dabler, & corroborates   230
with an opinion of mine which I have long formed,— that
Business & Fancy should be regarded as two things.

Censor. Ay, madam, & with one of mine which I hold to be
equally singular.

Mrs. Sapient. What is it, sir?

Censor. That London & Paris should be regarded as 2 Places.

Mrs. Sapient. Pshaw!

Codger *to Lady Smatter.* I say, madam, I am thinking—

Censor. Then, Sir, you are most worthily employed; & this
good Company desire nothing less than to impede the   240
progress of your thoughts, by troubling you to relate them.

Dabler. Very true; suppose, therefore, we change the subject.
[5v] O, apropos, have you seen the new verses that run
about?

Censor. No. Give me leave, madam, (*turning to Lady Smatter,*) to acquaint you with the motive of my present visit.—

Lady Smatter. You would not be such a Goth as to interrupt
our literary Discussions?— besides, I must positively have
your sentiments upon an argument I have just had with Mr.
Codger upon this Line of Pope   250
                    Most Women—

Censor. Hold, madam; I am no Quixote, & therefore en-
counter not danger where there is no prospect of reward;
nor shall I, till I emulate the fate of Orpheus, ever argue
about Women— in their presence.

Dabler. Ha, Ha! mighty well said. But <I was going to tell you,
Mr. Censor, that if you have any desire to look at those
Verses I was speaking of, I believe I have a Copy of them in
my Pocket. Let's see,— yes, here they are; how lucky that I
should happen to have them about me! (*gives them to*   260
Censor.) (*aside.*) I think they will surprise him.>

<*Censor reading.* That passion which we strongest feel
        We all agree to disapprove;
        Yet feebly, feebly we conceal—>

---

254 Orpheus, a priest of Apollo, angered women devoted to the worship of
Dionysus, who killed him by tearing him limb from limb.

<Dabler pettishly. Sir you read without any spirit,—
                    Yet feebly,— feebly we conceal
You should drop your Voice at the Second feebly, or you
lose all the effect. *(aside.)* It puts me in a Fever to [6r] hear
such fines lines murdered.>

<Censor reading. We all are bound slaves to self love.>   270

<Dabler snatching the Paper. Why you give it niether emphasis nor expression! you read as if you were asleep.
(reading.) That passion which—>

<Censor. O no more, no more of it. Pray who is the Author?>

<Dabler. Why really I— I don't absolutely know,— but, by
what I have heard, I should take it to be somebody very—
very clever.>

<Censor. You should?>

<Dabler. Yes: &, indeed, to own the truth, I have heard it
whispered that it is a posthumous Work of— of— O, of   280
Gay,— ay, of Gay.>

<Censor. Of Gay?>

<Dabler. Yes; found in a little corner of his private
Bureau.>

<Censor. And pray who has the impudence to make such an
assertion?>

<Dabler. Who?— o, as to that, really I don't know who in
particular,— but I assure you not *me*,— though, by the
way, do you really think it very bad?>

<Censor. Despicable beyond abuse. Are you not of the same   290
opinion?>

<Dabler. Me?— why, really, as to that— I— I can't exactly
say,— that is, I have hardly read it.— *[aside.]* What a
Crabbed fellow! there is not an ounce of Taste in his whole
composition. Curse me, if I was Nature, if I should not blush

256-297 There seem to be two stages of cuts in this extended passage. A
number of individual lines are marked for possible excision, but in addition,
the entire section is bracketed. It appears as though the individual lines were
marked first, and then later it was thought better to remove the entire passage. Whether the scene was being shortened for dramatic effect or whether
it was somehow objectionable is not clear.

to [6v] have made him. Hold, my Tablets! a good thought that! I'll turn it into a Lampoon, & drop it at Stapletons'.

(*walks aside & writes in his Tablets.*)>

Censor, to Lady Smatter. I have seen Miss Stanley, madam, &—

Lady Smatter. Did you find her at Mrs. Voluble's?

Censor. Yes. (*they whisper.*)   300

Mrs. Sapient, listening. (aside.) So, so, she's at Mrs. Voluble's!— there must certainly be some design upon Dabler.

Censor. But hear me, madam. I have something to communicate to you which—

Lady Smatter. Not now, I can attend to nothing now. These Evenings, Sir, which I devote to the fine arts, must not be contaminated with common affairs.

Mrs. Sapient. (*aside.*) I sha'n't rest till I have dived into this matter. [*to Lady Smatter.*] I am much chagrined, madam, at the disagreeable necessity I am under of breaking   310 abruptly from this learned & ingenious assembly, but I am called hence by an appointment which I cannot give up without extreme rudeness; & I must confess I should be rather sorry to be guilty of that, as I have long been of opinion that a breach of good manners— is no great sign of Politeness.

Lady Smatter. I am quite sorry to lose you so soon.

(***Exit Mrs. Sapient.***)

What a tiresome Creature! how glad I am she's gone!

Codger. Notwithstanding the rebuff I have just met with, madam, I must say I cannot help thinking that— [7r]   320

Censor. Do you mean, Sir, to satirize the whole Company, that you thus repeatedly profess thinking among those who have no other aim than talking?

Codger. Sir when a man has been pondering upon a Subject for a considerable Time, & assorting his ideas in order to explain himself, it is an exceedingly uncivil thing to interrupt him.

---

297 Stapletons': Apparently meant to be a coffee-house, where pamphlets, newspapers, and other reading materials were always to be found. Bryant Lillywhite's *London Coffee Houses* (London: George Allen and Unwin, 1963) does not catalogue a Stapletons'.

Lady Smatter. Mr. Dabler, what are you writing?

Dabler. Only a little memorandum, ma'am, about business; nothing more.   330

Codger. (*aside.*) I find I can never get in 2 Words at a Time.

Enter Jack.

Jack. Ma'am your Ladyship's most obedient.

Lady Smatter. Why did not you come sooner, Jack?— we are just broke up.

Jack. I could not help it, upon my word. I came away now just as my Tea was poured out at the Coffee House, because I would not stay to Drink it.

Codger. (*aside.*) I'm glad Jack's come; I think, at least, I shall make him listen to me.   340

Jack. I have been in such a hurry the whole Day, that I have never known what I have been about. I believe I have been to 16 places since Dinner. You good folks who sit here talking by the Hour together, must lead strange dull Lives; I wonder you don't lose the use of your Limbs.

Codger. Son Jack, when you have finished your Speech, please to [7v] hear one of mine.

Jack. I hope it won't be a long one, Sir.

Codger. Why do you hope that, Son, before you know how well it may entertain you?   350

Jack. Lord, Sir, I never think of being entertained with speeches.

Codger. What, Jack, not with your own Father's?

Jack. Lord no, Sir.

Codger. No, Sir? and pray, Sir, Why?

Jack. Because I'm always tired before they're half done.

Codger. Son Jack, 'tis these loose Companions that you keep that teach you all this profligacy. Tired of hearing me speak! one would think the poor Lad was an Ideot.

Jack. So this is your Club Room, where you all meet to talk?   360

Censor. Yes; & the principal maxim of the learned members is That no one shall listen to what is said by his neighbour.

Lady Smatter. Fie, Mr. Censor, I'm sure we're all attention—

Censor. Yes, to sieze the next opportunity of speaking.

Lady Smatter. Never mind what Mr Censor says, Jack, for you know he is a professed Stoic.

Censor. Stoic? pray what does your Ladyship mean?

Lady Smatter. Well, well, Cynic, then, if you like it better.

Censor. You hold, then, that their signification is the same?

Lady Smatter. Mercy, Mr. Censor, do you expect me to de-   370
fine the exact meaning of every word I make use of?

Censor. No, madam, not unless I could limit your Ladyship's Language to the Contents of a Primer. [8r]

Lady Smatter. O horrid! did you ever hear any thing so splenetic? Mr. Dabler, what are you Writing? Suppose, in compliment to our new member, you were to indulge us with a few Lines?

Dabler. Does your Ladyship mean an Extempore?

Lady Smatter. The thing in the World I should like best.

Dabler. Really, ma'am, I wish for nothing upon Earth so   380
much as the honour of your Ladyship's Commands,— but
as to an Extempore— the amazing difficulty,— the genius
requisite,— the masterly freedom,— the— the— the things
of that sort it requires make me half afraid of so bold an Un-
dertaking.

Censor. Sir, your Exordium is of sufficient length.

Dabler. I shall but collect my thoughts, & be ready in a moment. In the mean Time, I beg I may not interrupt the Conversation; it will be no manner of disturbance to me to hear
you all talking; we Poets, ma'am, can easily detach our-   390
selves from the Company.

                                        (*Walks apart.*)

Censor. I should be glad if your Ladyship would inform me
what Time, according to the established regulations of your
Society, you allow for the *Study* of extemporary Verses?

366-368 *Stoic*: Originally a member of a Greek school of philosophers noted
for the austerity of their ethical doctrines, the word has come to mean "One
who practices repression of emotion, indifference to pleasure or pain, and
patient endurance." The *Cynics*, members of another Greek school of philosophy, were originally notable for an "ostentatious contempt for ease and
wealth or pleasure," but the word now describes people disposed to finding
fault (*OED*).

Lady Smatter. I think we have no fixed rule; some are quick, & some are slow,— 'tis just as it happens.

Censor. (*aside.*) What unconsious absurdity!

> (*while they are speaking,* **Dabler** *privately looks at a paper, which he accidentally drops instead of putting in his pocket.*) [8v]

Dabler advancing. I hope I have not detained you long?

Lady Smatter. Is it possible you can be ready so soon?

Dabler. O dear yes, ma'am; these little things are done in a moment; they cost *us* nothing.   400

> In one sole point agree we all,
> Both Rich & Poor, & Saint & Sinner,
> Proud or Humble, Short or Tall,—
> And that's— a taste for a good Dinner.

Lady Smatter. O charming! I never heard any thing so satirical in my Life.

Censor. And so, Sir, you composed these lines just now?

Dabler. This very moment.

Censor. It seems, then, you can favour your Friends whenever they call upon you?   410

Dabler. O yes, Sir, with the utmost pleasure.

Censor. I should be obliged to you, then, Sir, for something more.

Dabler. Sir you do me honour. I will but take an Instant for consideration, & endeavour to obey you. [(*aside.*)] so, so!— I thought I should bring him round at last!

> (*walking away.*)

Censor. Stay, Sir. As you make these Verses with so much facility, you can have no objection, I presume, to my chusing you a Subject?   420

Dabler. Sir!

Censor. And then with firmer courage your Friends may counter-act the scepticism of the Envious, & boldly affirm [9r] that they are your own, & unstudied.

Dabler. Really, Sir, as to that, I can't say I very much mind what those sort of people say; we authors, Sir, are so much inured to illiberal attacks, that we regard them as nothing,— mere marks, Sir, of celebrity, & hear them without the least emotion.

Censor. You are averse, then, to my proposal? 430

Dabler. O dear no, Sir!— not at all,— not in the least, I assure you, Sir! (*aside.*) I wish he was in the Deserts of Lybia with all my Heart!

Censor. The readiness of your compliance, Sir, proves the promptness of your Wit. I shall name a subject which, I believe, you will find no difficulty to dilate upon,— self-sufficiency.

Dabler. Sir?

Censor. Self-sufficiency,— don't you understand me?

Dabler. Really, Sir, in regard to that, I don't exactly know 440 whether I do or not, but I assure you if you imagine that *I* am self-sufficient, you are most prodigiously mistaken; I defy any body to charge me with that, for though I have written so many things that have pleased every body else, I have always made it a rule to keep my own opinion to myself. Even Mr. Codger must, in this point, do me justice. Will you not, sir?

Codger. Sir, I shall say nothing.

　　　　　(folds his arms, and leans upon the Table.)

Censor. Well, Sir, I will give you another Subject, then, for of this, I must own, you might long since have been [9v] 450 weary. I will not affront you by naming so hackneyed a theme as Love, but give us, if you please, a spirited Couplet upon War.

Dabler. Upon War?— hum— let's see,— upon War,— ay,— but hold! don't you think, Sir, that War is rather a disagreeable Subject where there are Ladies? For *myself* I can certainly have no objection, but, I must confess, I am rather in doubt whether it will be quite polite to Lady Smatter.

Jack. Why Lord, Mr. Dabler, a man might ride Ten Times round Hyde Park, before you are ready to begin. 460

Dabler. Sir you don't know what you talk of; things of this importance are not to be settled rashly.

---

439 Self-sufficiency: not necessarily synonymous with self-dependence; at this period a self-sufficient person might be described as "Having excessive confidence in oneself, one powers, etc.; characterized by over-weening or self-conceited opinion or behavior" (*OED*).

Censor. Mr. Dabler I will give you an opportunity of taking
your revenge; let your Verses be upon the use & abuse of
Time, & address them, if you please, to that Gentleman.

Jack. Ay, with all my Heart. He may address what he will to
me, so as he will not keep me long to hear him.

Dabler. Time, did you say?— the use & the abuse of Time?—
ay, very good, a very good subject,— Time?— yes, a very
good idea, indeed!— the use & the abuse of Time,—   470
(*Pauses.*) But pray, Sir, pray, Mr. Censor, let me Speak a
word to you; are you not of opinion— now don't imagine
this is any objection of *mine*, no, I like the subject of all
things,— it is just what I wished,— but don't you think that
poor Mr. Codger, here, may think it is meant as a sneer at
him?

Censor. How so, Sir? [10r]

Dabler. Why, Sir, on account of his being so slow. And really,
notwithstanding his old fashioned ways, one would not
wish to affront him, poor man, for he means no harm. Be-   480
sides, Sir, his age!— consider that; we ought all to make al-
lowances for the infirmities of age. I'm sure *I* do,— poor
old Soul!

Censor. Well, Sir, I shall name but one subject more, & to that
if you object, you must give me leave to draw my own infer-
ence from your backwardness, & to report it accordingly.

Dabler. Sir I shall be very— I shall be extremely— that is, Sir,
I shall be quite at your Service. (*aside.*) What a malignant
fellow!

Censor. What say you, Sir, to an Epigram on slander?   490

Dabler. On slander?

Censor. Yes, Sir; what objection can you devise to that?

Dabler. An illiberal Subject, Sir! a most illiberal subject,— I
will have nothing to do with it.

Censor. The best way to manifest your contempt will be to
satirize it.

Dabler. Why, as you say,— there's something in that;— satirize it?— ay, Satirize slander,— ha! ha! a good hit enough!

Censor. Then, Sir, you will favour us without further delay.

Dabler. Sir I should be extremely happy to obey you,— noth-   500
ing could give me greater pleasure, only that just now I am

so particularly pressed for Time, that I am obliged to run away. Lady Smatter, I have the honour [10v] to wish your Ladyship good night.   (*going.*)

Jack *stopping him.* Fair play, fair play! you sha'n't go till you have made the verses; or, if you do, I swear I'll run after you.

Dabler. Upon my word, Sir—

Censor. Prithee, Jack, don't detain him. This anecdote, you know, (*affecting to whisper,*) will *Tell* as well without the   510
Verses as with them.

Dabler. (*aside.*) That fellow is a mere compound of spite & envy.

Lady Smatter. Come, Mr. Dabler, I see you relent.

Dabler. Why,— hem!— if— if your Ladyship insists— pray, Mr. Censor, what is this same subject you have been talking of?

Censor. O, Sir, 'tis no matter; if you are so much hurried, why should you stay? we are all pretty well convinced of the alacrity of your wit already.   520

Dabler. Slander, I think it was?— but suppose, sir, for slander we substitute Fashion?— I have a notion I could do something upon Fashion.

Censor. Probably, Sir, you *have* done something upon Fashion; entertain us, therefore, upon the given subject, or else be a better nomenclator to your verses than to call them extemporary.

Dabler. Well, Sir, well!— (*aside & walking away.*) a surly fellow!

Jack. Pray has your Ladyship heard the queer Story about the   530
Miss Sippets?

Lady Smatter. No; what is it?

Jack. Why I heard it just now at Mrs. Gabble's. Sir [11r] Harry Frisk, you know, last Winter paid his addresses to the Eldest Sister, but this Winter, to make what variety he could without quitting the Family, he deserted to the Youngest; & this morning they were to have been married.

Lady Smatter. Well, & were they not?

Jack. Upon my Word I don't know.

Lady Smatter. Don't know? what do you mean?   540

Jack. Why I had not Time to enquire.

Lady Smatter. Pho, prithee, Jack, don't be so ridiculous.

Dabler, holding his Hand before his Eyes, & walking about. Not one thought,— not one thought to save me from ruin!

Censor. Why, Mr. Codger, what are you about? is it not rather melancholy to sit by yourself at the Table, & not join at all in the conversation?

Codger, raising his Head. Perhaps, Sir, I may conceive myself to be somewhat Slighted.

Lady Smatter. Nay, nay, prithee, my good friend, don't be so captious.   550

Codger. Madam I presume, at least, I have as good a right to be affronted as another man; for which reason—

Dabler pettishly. Upon my Word, if you all keep talking so incessantly, it is not possible for a man to know what he is about.

Codger. I have not spoken before for this half Hour, & yet I am as good as bid to hold my Tongue!

(*leans again on the Table.*) [11v]

Jack. O but, ma'am, I forgot to tell your Ladyship the very best part of the Story; the poor Eldest Sister was quite driven to despair, so last night, to avoid, at least, Dancing bare-foot at her Sister's Wedding, she made an appointment with a young Haberdasher in the neighbourhood to set off for Scotland.   560

Lady Smatter. Well?

Jack. Well, & when she got into the post chaise, instead of her new Lover the young Haberdasher, who do you think was waiting to receive her?

Lady Smatter. Nay, nay, tell me at once.

Jack. But who do you guess?   570

Lady Smatter. Pho, pho, don't be so tiresome. Who was it?

---

550 *Lady Smatter.*] Lady Smatter. *MS*

561–562 Dancing bare-foot: According to Margaret Baker's *Folklore and Customs of Rural England* (Totowa, New Jersey: Rowman and Littlefield, 1974), it was considered a social disgrace for an eldest daughter to be unmarried at the time of a younger sister's wedding, and in parts of England it was customary to make her advertise her state by performing a bare-foot dance after the wedding ceremony (140).

Jack. Why that I am not certain myself.

Lady Smatter. Not certain yourself?

Jack. No, for I had not Time to stay till Mrs. Gabble came to the Name.

Lady Smatter. How absurd!

Codger, again raising his Head. Madam if I might be allowed,— or, rather, to speak more properly, if I could get Time to give my opinion of this matter, I should say—

Lady Smatter. My good friend, we should all be extremely   580
happy to hear you, if you were not so long in coming to the point;— that's all the fault we find with you; is it not, Jack?

Jack. To be sure, ma'am. Why sometimes, do you know, I have made a Journey to Bath & back again, while [12r] he has been considering whether his next Wig should be a Bob, or a full-bottom.

Codger. Son Jack, this is very unseemly discourse, & I desire—

Lady Smatter. Nay, pray don't scold him. Jack, when shall you hear any more of Miss Sippet's adventure?

Jack. Why, ma'am, either to-morrow or Friday, I don't know   590
which.

Codger. (*aside, & reclining as before.*) I verily believe they'd rather hear Jack than me!

Jack. Why Lord, Mr. Dabler, I believe you are Dreaming. Will you never be ready?

Dabler. Sir this is really unconscionable! I was just upon the point of finishing,— & now you have put it all out of my Head!

Censor. Well, Mr. Dabler, we release you, now, from all further trouble, since you have sufficiently satisfied us that   600
your extempery verses are upon a new construction.

Dabler. O, Sir, as to that, making verses is no sort of *trouble* to me, I assure you,— however, if you don't chuse to hear these which I have been composing—

---

575 Name] *cor, original word illegible*
586 Bob or a full-bottom: A Bob wig had short locks turned under at the end; a full-bottom was longer, fuller, and curlier. Bob wigs were in fashion at the time: Janet Arnold, *Perukes and Periwigs* (London: Her Majesty's Stationery Office, 1970), 19–21.

Lady Smatter. O but *I* do, so pray—

Jack. Pho, pho, he has not got them ready.

Dabler. You are mistaken, Sir, these are quite ready,— entirely finished,— & lodged here; (*-pointing to his Head,-*)
but as Mr Censor—

Censor. Nay, if they are ready, you may as well repeat them.   610

Dabler. No, Sir, no, since you declined hearing them at first, I
am above compelling you to hear them at all. [12v] Lady
Smatter, the next Time I have the honour of seeing your
Ladyship, I shall be proud to have your opinion of them.

(Exit hastily.)

Censor. Poor Wretch! "Glad of a Quarrel strait he shuts the
Door,"— what's this? (*picks up the Paper dropt by Dabler,-*)
so! so! so!—

Enter Beaufort.

Beaufort *to Lady Smatter.* Pardon me, madam, if I interrupt you, I am come but for a moment. Censor, (*apart to*
Censor,-) have you no heart? are you totally divested of   620
humanity?

Censor. Why what's the matter?

Beaufort. The matter? You have kept me on the Rack,— you
have wantonly tortured me with the most intolerable suspence that the mind of Man is capable of enduring. Where
is Cecilia?— have you given her my message?— have you
brought me any answer?— why am I kept in ignorance of
every thing I wish or desire to know?

Censor. Is your Harangue finished?

Beaufort. No, Sir, it is hardly begun! This unfeeling propen-   630
sity to raillery upon occasions of serious distress, is cruel, is
unjustifiable, is insupportable. No Man could practice it,
whose Heart was not hardened against pity, Friendship,
Sorrow,— & every kind, every endearing tie by which the
Bonds of Society are united.

---

607 these] there *MS*

612 all. / Lady] all. La- / -dy *MS*

615–616 Glad . . . door: a paraphrase of Pope's "An Epistle To Dr. Arbuth-
not," published in 1735: "Glad of a quarrel, strait I clapt the door" (*Poems*,
4:100, line 67).

Censor. At least, my good friend, object not to rallery in me,
till you learn to check railing in yourself. I would fain know
by what Law or what Title you Gentlemen of the Sighing
Tribe assume the exclusive privelege of [13r] appropriating
all severities of Speech to yourselves.   640

Lady Smatter. Beaufort, your behaviour involves me in the
utmost confusion. After an Education such as I have bestowed upon you, this weak anxiety about mere private affairs is unpardonable;— especially in the presence of people of learning.

Beaufort. I waited, madam, till Mrs. Sapient and Mr. Dabler
were gone,— had I waited longer, patience must have de-
generated into insensibility. From your Ladyship & from
Mr. Codger, my anxiety has some claim to indulgence,
since it's cause is but too well known to you both.   650

Jack. [*aside.*] Not a word of me! I'll e'en sneak away before
he finds me out.   (*going.*)

Codger. Son Jack, please to Stop.

Jack. Sir I can't; my Time's expired.

Codger. Son, if I conceive aright, your Time, properly Speaking, ought to be mine.

Jack. Lord, Sir, only look at my Watch; it's just 8 o'clock, & I
promised Billy Skip to call on him before 7 to go to the
Play.

Codger. Son Jack, it is by no means a dutiful principle you are   660
proceeding upon, to be fonder of the Company of Billy
Skip than of your own Father.

Beaufort. For mercy's sake, Sir, debate this point some other
Time. Censor, why will you thus deny me all information?

Codger. So it is continually! whenever I speak you are all
sure to be in a hurry! Jack, come hither & sit by me; *you*
[13v] may hear me, I think, if nobody else will. Sit down, I
say.

Jack. Lord, Sir—

Codger. Sit down when I bid you, & listen to what I am going   670
to tell you.

   (*Makes Jack seat himself at the Table, & talks to him.*)

_____

664 information?] ~ . MS

Lady Smatter. Beaufort, let *me* speak to Mr. Censor. what
have you done, Sir, about this poor Girl? did you give her
my message?

Censor. She had too much Sense, too much Spirit, too much
dignity to hear it.

Lady Smatter. Indeed?

Censor. Yes; & therefore I should propose—

Lady Smatter. Sir, I must beg you not to interfere in this
transaction; it is not that I mean to doubt either your   680
knowledge or your learning, far from it,— but nevertheless
I must presume that I am myself as competent a Judge of
the matter as you can be, since I have reason to believe—
you'll excuse me, sir,— that I have read as many Books as
you have.

Beaufort. O those eternal Books! what, madam, in the name
of reason, & of common Sense, can Books have to do in
such an affair as this?

Lady Smatter. How? do you mean to depreciate Books? to
doubt their general utility, & universal influence? Beaufort,   690
I shall Blush to own you for my Pupil! Blush to recollect the
fruitless efforts with which I have laboured, as Shakespeare
finely says,

>   To teach the young idea how to shoot.—

Censor. Shakespeare?— then what a Thief was Thompson!
[14r]

Lady Smatter. Thompson? O, ay, true, now I recollect, so it
was.

Censor. Nay, madam, it little matters which, since both, you
know, were authors.   700

Beaufort. Unfeeling Censor! is this a Time to divert yourself
with satirical dryness? defer, I conjure you, these useless,
idle, ludicrous disquisitions, &, for a few moments, suffer affairs of real interest & importance to be heard & understood.

---

694 To teach . . . shoot: James Thomson (1700-1748) published a cycle of
four poems titled *The Seasons* in 1730. This line is from part I, "Spring"
(*The Seasons.* ed. James Sambrook [Oxford: Clarendon Press, 1981], 55, line
1153).
699 *Censor.*] Censor. *MS*

Lady Smatter. Beaufort, you expose yourself more & more every Word you utter; disquisitions which relate to Books & authors ought never to be deferred. Authors, Sir, are the noblest of human Beings, & Books—

Beaufort. Would to Heaven there were not one in the World!

Lady Smatter. O monstrous!   710

Beaufort. Once again, madam, I entreat, I conjure—

Lady Smatter. I will not hear a Word more. Wish there was not a Book in the World? Monstrous, shocking, & horrible! Beaufort, you are a lost Wretch! I tremble for your Intellects; & if you do not speedily conquer this degenerate passion, I shall abandon you without remorse to that Ignorance & Depravity to which I see you are plunging.   *(Exit.)*[14v]

Beaufort & Censor. Codger & Jack at the Table.

Beaufort. Hard-Hearted, vain, ostentatious Woman! Go, then, & leave me to that Independance which not all your smiles could make me cease to regret! Censor, I am weary of this   720 contention; what is Life, if the Present must continually be sacrificed to the Future? I will fly to Cecilia, & I will tear myself from her no more. If, without Her, I can receive no happiness, why, with Her, should I be apprehensive of misery?

Censor. know you not, Beaufort, that if you Sap the foundation of a Structure, 'tis madness to expect the Sides & the top will stand self-supported? Is not security from want the Basis of all Happiness? & if you undermine that, do you not lose all possibility of enjoyment? Will the presence of Cecilia soften the hardships of Penury? Will her Smiles teach   730 you to forget the pangs of Famine? Will her Society make you insensible to the severities of an Houseless Winter?

Beaufort. Well, well, tell me where I can find her, & she shall direct my future conduct herself.

Censor. I have a Scheme upon Lady Smatter to communicate to you, which, I think, has some chance of succeeding.

Beaufort. Till I have seen Cecilia, I can attend to nothing; [15r] once more, tell me where she is.

---

723 I can receive] I can *<deleted indecipherable word>* receive
724 Her] *cor, lc or*

Censor. Where-ever she is, she has more wisdom than her
Lover, for she charged me to command your absence.   740
Beaufort. My absence?
Censor. Nay, nay, I mean not seriously to suppose the Girl is
wise enough to wish it; however, if she pretends to desire
it, you have a sufficient excuse for non-attendance.
Beaufort. I don't understand you.— Is Cecilia offended?
Censor. Yes, & most marvellously, for niether herself nor her
Neighbors know why.
Beaufort. I will not stay another minute!— I will find other
methods to discover her abode.   (*going.*)
Censor. Prithee, Beaufort, be less absurd. My scheme upon   750
Lady Smatter—
Beaufort. I will not hear it! I disdain Lady Smatter, & her fu-
ture smiles or displeasure shall be equally indifferent to me.
Too long, already, have I been governed by motives &
Views which level me with her narrow-minded self; it is
Time to shake off the yoke,— assert the freedom to which I
was Born,— & dare to be Poor, that I may learn to be
Happy!   (*Exit.*)
Censor. Shall this noble fellow be suffered to ruin himself?
no! the World has too few like him. Jack, a word with-   760
you,— Jack, I say!— are you asleep, man?
Codger. Asleep? Surely not.
Censor. If you're awake, answer!
Jack, yawning. Why what's the matter?[15v]
Censor. Wake, man, wake & I'll tell you.
Codger. How, asleep? pray, Son Jack, what's the reason of
your going to Sleep when I'm talking to you?
Jack. Why, Sir, I have so little Time for Sleep, that I thought I
might as well take the opportunity.
Codger. Son Jack, Son Jack, you are verily an Ignoramus!   770
Censor. Come hither, Jack. I have something to propose to
you—
Codger. Sir I have not yet done with him myself. Where-
abouts was I, Son, when you fell asleep?
Jack. Why there, Sir, where you are now.
Codger. Son you are always answering like a Blockhead; I
mean whereabouts was I in my Story?

Jack. What story, Sir?

Codger. How? did not you hear my story about your aunt
    Deborah's Poultry?   780

Jack. Lord, no, Sir!

Codger. Not hear it? why what were you thinking of?

Jack. Me, Sir? why how many places I've got to go to to-night.

Codger. This is the most indecorous behaviour I ever saw.
    You don't deserve ever to hear me tell a story again. Pray,
    Mr. Censor, did *you* hear it?

Censor. No.

Codger. Well, then, as it's a very good Story, I think I'll e'en
    take the trouble to tell it once more. You must know, then,
    my Sister Deborah, this silly Lad's aunt—   790

Censor. Mr. Codger I am too much engaged to hear you
    now,— I have Business that calls me away.

Codger. This is always the Case! I don't think I ever Spoke to
    3 Persons in my Life that did not make some pretence for
    leaving me [16r] before I had done!

Censor. Jack, are you willing to serve your Brother?

Jack. That I am! I would ride to York to see what's O'Clock
    for him.

Censor. I will put you in a way to assist him with less trouble,
    though upon a matter of at least equal importance. You,   800
    too, *Mr. Codger,* have, I believe, a good regard for him?

Codger. Sir I shall beg leave to decline making any answer.

Censor. Why so, Sir?

Codger. Because, Sir, I never intend to utter a Word more in
    this Room; but, on the contrary, it is my intention to aban-
    don the Club from this Time forward.

Censor. But is that any reason why you should not answer
    me?

Codger. Sir I shall quit the place directly; for I think it an ex-
    tremely hard thing to be made speak when one has nothing 810
    to say, & hold one's Tongue when one has got a speech
    ready.   *(Exit.)*

797-798 "ride to York . . .": In the seventeenth century several legends arose
concerning highwaymen who committed crimes and then established alibis
by desperately riding to York, arriving before the clock struck a certain hour,
thereby appearing to have been in York when the crime occurred.

Jack. Is he gone? huzza! I was never so tired in my life.

(going.)

Censor. Hold! I have something to say to you.

Jack. Can't possibly stay to hear you.

Censor. Prithee, Jack, how many Duels do you fight in a year?

Jack. Me? Lord, not one.

Censor. How many Times, then, do you beg pardon to escape a Caning?

Jack. a Caning?   820

Censor. Yes; or do you imagine the very wildness & inattention by which you offend, are competent to make your apology?

Jack. Lord, Mr. Censor, you are never easy but when you are asking some queer Question! But I don't much mind you. you odd sort of People, who do nothing all Day but *muz* yourselves with thinking, are always coming out with these sort of trimmers; however, I know you so well, that they make no impression on me.   (*Exit.*)

Censor. Through what a multiplicity of Channels does Folly   830
glide! it's Streams, alternately turgid, calm, rapid & lazy, take their several Directions from the peculiarities of the minds whence they Spring,— frequently varying in their Courses,— but ever similar in their Shallowness!

End. of ACT 4 [16v]

---

826 *muz*: apparent corruption of *amuse*, but no other recorded use discovered.

828 trimmers: one who or that which reproves or reprimands (*OED*)

835 **End. of ACT 4**] **End. oE** ~ MS.

Act V.

S c e n e *a Parlour at Mrs. Voluble's.*

Mrs. Voluble, Mrs. Wheedle, Miss Jenny & Bob
are seated at a round Table at Supper;
***Betty** is waiting.*

Mrs. Voluble. Well, this is a sad thing indeed!— Betty, give
me some Beer. Come, Miss Jenny, here's your Love & mine.
(*Drinks.*)

Mrs. Wheedle. I do believe there's more misfortunes in our
way of Business than in any in the World; the fine Ladies
have no more conscience than a Jew,— they keep ordering
& ordering, & think no more of paying than if one could
Live upon a needle & Thread.

Mrs. Voluble. Ah, the Times are very bad! very bad, indeed!— all the Gentlefolks breaking,— why, Betty, the   10
meat i'n't half done!— poor Mr. Mite, the rich cheesemonger at the Corner is quite knocked up.

Mrs. Wheedle. You don't say so?

Mrs. Voluble. Very true, indeed.

Mrs. Wheedle. Well, who'd have thought of that? Pray, Mrs.
Betty, give me some Bread.

Miss Jenny. Why it is but a Week a go that I met him a dri-
ving his own Whiskey.

Mrs. Voluble. Ah, this is a sad World! a very sad World, indeed! nothing but ruination going forward [2r] from one   20

11-12 Mr. Mite . . . is quite knocked up: the *OED* lists *mite* as a slang word
for cheesemonger as early as the 1760s; it also includes a citation from the
Dictionary of the Vulgar Tongue, published in 1785 by Francis Grose
(1731?-1791), defining *mite* as "a nick name for a cheesemonger, from the
small insect of that name found in cheese." To knock up is to "break up, destroy, put an end to" (*OED*).
18 Whiskey: "a kind of light two-wheeled one-horse carriage, used in England and America in the late 18th and early 19th c." (*OED*).

end of the Town to the other. My dear Mrs. Wheedle, you don't Eat; pray let me help you to a little Slice more.

Mrs. Wheedle. O, I shall do very well; I only wish you'd take care of yourself.

Mrs. Voluble. There, that little bit can't hurt you, I'm sure. As to Miss Jenny, she's quite like a Crocodile, for she Lives upon air.

Mrs. Wheedle. No, ma'am, the thing is she Laces so tight, that she can't Eat half her natural victuals.

Mrs. Voluble. Ay, ay, that's the way with all the Young   30
Ladies; they pinch for fine shapes.

Bob. Mother, I wish you'd help *me*,— I'm just starved.

Mrs. Voluble. Would you have me help you before I've helped the Company, you greedy fellow, you? Stay till we've done, can't you? & then if there's any left, I'll give you a bit.

Miss Jenny. I'll give Master Bobby a piece of mine, if you please, ma'am.

Mrs. Voluble. No, no, he can't be very hungry, I'm sure, for he Eat a Dinner to frighten a Horse. And so, as I was telling you, she has agreed to stay here all night, & to be sure, poor   40
Thing, she does nothing in the World but Cry, all as ever I can say to her, & I believe I was talking to her for a matter of an Hour before you came, without her making so much as a word of answer. I declare it makes one as melancholy as a Cat to see her. I think this is the nicest cold Beef I [2v] ever Tasted,— you *must* Eat a bit, or I shall take it quite ill.

Mrs. Wheedle. Well, it must be *leetle* tiny morsel, then.

Mrs. Voluble. I shall cut you quite a *fox-hall* slice.

26-27 Crocodile . . . Lives upon air: Mrs. Voluble probably means chameleon, which, " . . . from their inanimate appearance, . . . were formerly supposed to live on air" (*OED*).

44 melancholy as a Cat: from Shakespeare's *1 Henry 4* (1597): "I am as melancholy as a gib cat or a lugg'd bear" (1.2.73-74. *Riverside Shakespeare*, 849).

48 *fox-hall slice*: The pleasure garden at Vauxhall was sometimes vulgarly referred to as the Fox-hall garden (*OED*); its waiters were famous for the thinness with which they could slice meat (James Granville Southworth, *Vauxhall Gardens: A Chapter in the Social History of England* [New York: Columbia University Press, 1941], 34).

Bob. Mother, if Mrs. Wheedle's had enough, you'd as good give it me. 50

Mrs. Voluble. I declare I don't believe there's such another fellow in the World for gormondizing!— There,— take that, & be quiet. So, as I was saying—

Bob. Lord, Mother, you've given me nothing but fat!

Mrs. Voluble. Ay, & too good for you, too. I think, at your age, you've no right to know fat from lean.

Mrs. Wheedle. Ah, Master Bobby, these are no Times to be dainty! one ought to be glad to get Bread to Eat. I'm sure, for my part, I find it as hard to get my Bills paid, as if the fine Ladies had no money but what they earned. 60

Mrs. Voluble. If you'll take my advice, Mrs. Wheedle, you'll send in your account directly, & then, if the young lady has any money left, you'll get it at once.

Mrs. Wheedle. Why that's just what I thought myself, so I made out the Bill, & brought it in my Pocket.

Mrs. Voluble. That's quite right. But, good [luck], Mrs. Wheedle, who'd have thought of such a young lady's being brought to such a pass?— I shall begin soon to think there's no trusting in any body.

Miss Jenny. For my part, if I was to chuse, I should like best 70 to be a Lady at once, & follow no Business at all. [3r]

Bob. And for my part, I should like best to be a Duke.

Mrs. Voluble. A Duke? you a Duke, indeed! you great numscull I wish you'd learn to hold your Tongue. I'll tell you what, Mrs. Wheedle, you must know it's my notion this young lady expects something in the money way out of the City, for she gave me a Letter, just before you came, to send by a Porter; so as I was coming down Stairs, I just peeped in at the Sides—

           Enter Cecilia.

O Law!— I hope she did not hear me! 80

Cecilia. I beg your pardon, Mrs. Voluble for this intrusion, but I rang my Bell 3 Times, & I believe nobody heard it.

---

49 **Bob.**] Bob. *MS*

77 the City: The city of London, in particular the business center and financial district, centered near the intersection of Poultry and Cornhill Streets.

Mrs. Voluble. I'm sure, ma'am, I'm quite sorry you've had such a trouble; but I dare say it was all my son Bobby's fault, for he keeps such a continual Jabbering, that there's no hearing any thing in the World for him.

Bob. Lord, Mother, I'll take my Oath I ha'n't spoke 3 words the whole Time! I'm sure I've done nothing but knaw that nasty fat this whole night.

Mrs. Voluble. What, you are beginning again, are you?—   90

Cecilia. I beg I may occasion no disturbance; I merely wished to know if my messenger were returned.

Mrs. Voluble. Dear no, ma'am, not yet.

Cecilia. Then he has certainly met with some accident. If you will be so good as to lend me your Pen & Ink once more, I will send another man after him.

Mrs. Voluble. Why, ma'am, he could not have got back so soon, let him go never so fast. [3v]

Cecilia, walking apart. So Soon! Oh how unequally are we affected by the progress of Time! Winged with the gay   100 Plumage of Hope, how rapid seems it's flight,— oppressed with the Burden of Misery, how tedious it's motion!— yet it varies not,— insensible to Smiles, & callous to Tears, it's acceleration & it's tardiness are mere phantasms of our disordered Imaginations. How strange that that which in it's course is most steady & uniform, should, to our deluded Senses, seem most mutable & irregular!

Miss Jenny. I believe she's talking to herself.

Mrs. Voluble. Yes, she has a mighty way of Musing. I have a good mind to ask her to Eat a bit, for, poor Soul, I dare say   110 she's hungry enough. Bobby, get up, & let her have your chair.

Bob. What, & then a'n't I to have any more?

Mrs. Voluble. Do as you're bid, will you, & be quiet. I declare I believe you think of nothing but Eating & Drinking all Day long. Ma'am, will it be agreeable to you to Eat a bit of Supper with us?

99–107 Cecilia's speech parodies the "high style." See Burney's *Early Journals and Letters* (1: 4) for a similar parody.

Mrs. Wheedle. The young lady does not hear you; I'll go to her myself. (*Rises & follows Cecilia.*) I hope, Miss Stanley, you're very well? I hope my lady's well? I believe, ma'am,   120 you don't recollect me?

Cecilia. Mrs. Wheedle?— yes, I do.

Mrs. Wheedle. I'm very sorry, I'm sure, ma'am, to hear of your misfortunes, but I hope things a'n't quite so bad as they're reported?

Cecilia. I thank you. Mrs. Voluble, is your Pen & Ink here? [4r]

Mrs. Voluble. You shall have it directly; but pray, ma'am, let me persuade you to Eat a morsel first.

Cecilia. I am obliged to you, but I cannot.   130

Mrs. Voluble. Why now here's the nicest little miniken bit you ever saw;— it's enough to tempt you to look at it.

Bob. Mother, if the lady don't like it, can't you give it me?

Mrs. Voluble. I was just this minute going to help you, but now you're so greedy, you sha'n't have a bit.

Cecilia. Mrs. Voluble, can I find the Pen & Ink myself?

Mrs. Voluble. I'll fetch it in 2 minutes. But, dear ma'am, don't fret, for bad things of one Sort or other are always coming to pass; & as to Breaking, & so forth, why I think it happens to every body. I'm sure there's Mr. Grease, the Tallow   140 Chandler, one of my most particular acquaintance, that's got as genteel a Shop as any in all London, is quite upon the very point of ruination: & Miss Moggy Grease, his Daughter—

Cecilia. I'll Step up Stairs, & when you are at leisure, you will be so good as to send me the Standish.   (*going.*)

Mrs. Wheedle, *stopping her.* Ma'am, as I did not know when I might have the pleasure of seeing you again, I took the liberty just to make out my little account, & bring it in my Pocket; & I hope, ma'am, that when you make up your af-   150 fairs, you'll be so good as to let me be the first Person that's considered, for I'm a deal out of Pocket, & should be very glad to have some of the money as soon as possible.

---

146 standish: "A stand containing ink, pens and other writing materials and accessories . . . " (*OED*).

148 up] *ins*, out *del*

Cecilia. Dunned already! good Heaven, what will [4v] become of me! (*bursts into Tears.*)

Mrs. Voluble. Dear ma'am, what signifies fretting?— better Eat a bit of Supper, & get up your Spirits. Betty, go for a clean Plate.   (*Exit Betty.*)

Mrs. Wheedle. Won't you please, ma'am, to look at the Bill?

Cecilia. Why should I look at it?— I cannot pay it,— I am a   160
destitute Creature,— without Friend or resource!

Mrs. Wheedle. But, ma'am, I only mean—

Cecilia. No matter what you mean!— all application to *me* is fruitless,— I possess nothing— The Beggar who sues to you for a Penny is not more powerless & wretched,— a tortured & insulted Heart is all that I can call my own!

Mrs. Wheedle. But sure, ma'am, when there comes to be a Division among your Creditors, your Debts won't amount to more than—

Cecilia. Forbear, forbear!— I am not yet inured to Disgrace, &   170
this manner of stating my affairs is insupportable. *Your* Debt, assure yourself, is secure, for sooner will I famish with want, or perish with Cold,— faint with the fatigue of labour, or consume with unassisted Sickness, than appropriate to my own use the smallest part of my shattered Fortune, till your— & every other claim upon it is answered. [5r]

Mrs. Wheedle. Well, ma'am, that's as much as one can expect.

Re-enter Betty, with a Plate & a Letter.

Betty. Ma'am is your name Miss Stanley?

Cecilia. Yes; is that Letter for me? (*takes it.*)

Mrs. Voluble. Betty why did not you bring the Letter first to   180
me? Sure I'm the Mistress of my own House. Come, Mrs. Wheedle, come & finish your supper.

(*Mrs. Wheedle returns to the Table.*)

Cecilia. I dread to open it! Does any body wait?

Betty. Yes, ma'am, a man in a fine Lace Livery.

Cecilia, *reading.* "Since you would not hear my message
"from Mr. Censor, I must try if you will read it from
"myself. I do most earnestly exhort you to go instantly
"& privately into the Country, & you may then depend upon

---

154 what will/ become of] what will [*catchword* become] / of MS
185 "Since ~] Since ~ MS

"my Support & protection. Beaufort now begins to listen
"to reason—"   190
        Oh Heaven!
"and, therefore, if you do not continue in Town with a
"view to attract his notice, or, by acquainting him with
"your retirement, seduce him to follow you—"
        Insolent, injurious Woman!
"I have no doubt but he will be guided by one whose
"experience & studies entitle her to direct him. I shall
"call upon you very soon, to know your determination, &
"to supply you with Cash for your Journey, being, with
"the utmost sorrow for your misfortunes, Dear Miss   200
"Stanley,
        "Yours & c   Judith Smatter."
        What a Letter! [5v]
Betty. Ma'am, if you please, is there any answer?
Cecilia. No, none.
Betty. Then, ma'am, what am I to say to the Footman?
Cecilia. Nothing.— yes,— tell him I have read *this* Letter, but
    if he brings me another, it will be returned unopened.
Betty. Yes, ma'am. Laws! what a comical answer!   (***Exit.***)
Mrs. Voluble. I wonder who that Letter was from!   210
Miss Jenny. I dare say I can guess. I'll venture something it's
    from her Sweetheart.
Mrs. Voluble. That's just my Thought! (*they whisper.*)
Cecilia. Is then every Evil included in poverty? & is the depri-
    vation of Wealth what is has least to regret? Are Contempt,
    Insult, & Treachery it's necessary attendants?— Is not the
    loss of affluence sufficiently bitter,— the ruin of all Hope
    sufficiently severe, but that Reproach, too, must add her
    Stings, & Scorn her Daggers?
Mrs. Voluble. When I've Eat this, I'll ask her if we guessed   220
    right.
Cecilia. "Beaufort begins to listen to reason,"— mercenary
    Beaufort! Interest has taken sole possession of thy Heart,—
    weak & credulous that I was to believe I had ever any share
    in it!

---

200 utmost] *ins*, greatest *del*

Mrs. Voluble. I'm of ten minds whether to speak to her, or leave her to her own Devices.

Cecilia. "To listen to reason,"— is, then, reason another word for baseness, falsehood & Inconstancy?

Mrs. Wheedle. I only wish my money was once safe in my Pocket. [6r]   230

Cecilia. Attract his notice? seduce him to follow!— am I already so Sunk? already regarded as a designing, interested wretch? I cannot bear the imputation,— my swelling Heart seems too big for it's mansion,— O that I could quit them all!

Mrs. Voluble rising & approaching Cecilia. Ma'am, I'm quite sorry to see you in such trouble; I'm afraid that Letter did not bring you agreeable news;— I'm sure I wish I could serve you with all my Heart, & if you're distressed about a Lodging, I've just thought of one in Queen Street, that, in a   240 week's Time,—

Cecilia. In a week's Time I hope to be far away from Queen Street,— far away from this hated City,— far away, if possible, from all to whom I am known!

Mrs. Voluble. Dear ma'am, sure you don't think of going beyond Seas?

Mrs. Wheedle. If you should like, ma'am, to go abroad, I believe I can help you to a thing of that sort myself.

Cecilia. How?

Mrs. Wheedle. Why, ma'am, I know a Lady who's upon the   250 very point of going, & the young Lady who was to have been her Companion, all of a sudden married a young Gentleman of Fortune, & left her without any notice.

Cecilia. Who is the lady?

Mrs. Wheedle. Mrs. Hollis, ma'am; she's a Lady of very good fortunes.

Cecilia. I have heard of her.

Mrs. Wheedle. And she wants a young lady very much. She [6v] sets off the beginning of next week. If it's agreeable to you to go to her, I shall be proud to shew you the way.   260

233 interested: "self-seeking, self-interested" (*OED*).
240 There were several Queen Streets in London, and all were near streets named King and Charles (see note to 3.2. 250–51).
258 *Mrs. Wheedle*] Mrs. Wheedle *MS*

Cecilia. I know not what to do!

Mrs. Voluble. Dear ma'am, I would not have you think of such a Desperation Scheme; things may be better soon, & who knows but Mr. Beaufort may prove himself a true Lover at the last? Lord, if you could but once get the Sight of him, I dare say, for all my lady, the Day would be your own.

Cecilia. What odious interpretations! to what insults am I exposed!— yes, I had indeed better quit the kingdom,— Mrs. Wheedle, I am ready to attend you.

Mrs. Wheedle. Then, Master Bobby, bid Betty call a Coach.   270

Cecilia. No,— stay!—

Mrs. Wheedle. What, ma'am, won't you go?

Cecilia, walking apart. Am I not too rash?— expose myself, like a common Servant, to be Hired?— submit to be examined, & hazard being rejected!— no, no, my Spirit is not yet so broken.

Mrs. Voluble. I hope, ma'am, you are thinking better of it. For my part, if I might be free to advise you, I should say send to the young Gentleman, & see first what is to be done with *him*.   280

Cecilia. What humiliating suggestions! yes, I see I must be gone,— I see I must hide myself from the World, or Submit to be suspected of Views & Designs I disdain to think of. Mrs. Wheedle, I cannot well accompany you to this Lady myself, but if you will go to her in my name,— tell her my unhappy situation, as far as your knowledge [7r] of it goes— & that, alas, includes but half it's misery!— you will much oblige me. When did you say she leaves England?

Mrs. Wheedle. Next week, ma'am.

Cecilia. I shall have Time, then, to arrange my affairs. Tell her   290 I know not, yet, in what capacity to offer myself, but that, at all events, it is my first wish to quit this Country.

Mrs. Wheedle. Yes, ma'am. I'll get my Hat & cloak, & go directly.   (*Exit.*)

Cecilia. Alas, to what abject dependance may I have exposed myself!

Mrs. Voluble. Come, ma'am, let me persuade you to Taste my Raison Wine,— I do believe it's the best that—

Cecilia. I thank you, but I can niether Eat nor Drink. (*going.*)

Re-enter **Mrs. Wheedle.**

Mrs. Wheedle. I suppose, ma'am, I may tell Mrs. Hollis you   300
   will have no objection to doing a little Work for the Children, & things of that sort, as the last young lady did?

Cecilia. Oh heavy Hour!— down, down, proud Heart!— Tell
   her what you will!— I must submit to my fate, not chuse it;
   & should servility & dependance be my lot, I trust, at least,
   that I shall not only find them new,— not only find them
   Heart-breaking & cruel— but short & expeditious.

Mrs. Voluble. But, ma'am, had not you best— [7v]

Cecilia. I have no more directions to give, & I can answer no
   more Questions. The sorrows of my situation seem every   310
   moment to be aggravated,— Oh Beaufort! faithless, unfeeling Beaufort! to have rescued you from distress & mortifica-
   tion such as this would have been my Heart's first joy,—
   my life's only pride!   (*Exit.*)

Mrs. Voluble. She's quite in a sad taking, that's the truth of it.

Miss Jenny. Poor young lady! I'm so sorry for her you can't
   think.

Mrs. Voluble. Come, Mrs. Wheedle, you sha'n't go till you've
   drunk a Glass of Wine, so let's sit down a little while & be
   comfortable. (*They seat themselves at the Table.*) you need   320
   not be afraid of the dark, for Bobby shall go with you.

Bob. Mother, I'd rather behalf not.

Mrs. Voluble. Who wants to know whether you'd rather or
   not? I suppose there's no need to consult all your rather-
   nesses. Well, Ma'am, so, as I was going to tell you, poor
   Miss Moggy Grease— (*A violent knocking at the Door.*)
   Lord bless me, who's at the Door? why they'll knock the
   House down! Somebody to Mr. Dabler, I suppose; but he
   won't be Home this 2 Hours.

Bob. Mother, may I help myself to a drop of Wine?   330
                                        (*Takes the Bottle.*)

Mrs. Voluble. Wine, indeed! no,— give me the Bottle this

---

301 Work: in such a feminine context, *work* would almost certainly refer to
needlework, "a distinctly feminine occupation" (*OED*).
322 behalf: by half, or "for my part" (Johnson, *Dictionary*).
326 Moggy] *lc MS*

minute. (*snatches & overturns it.*) look here, you nasty fellow, [8r] see how you've made me spill it!

Enter Betty.

Betty. Laws, ma'am, here's a fine lady all in her Coach, & she
asks for nobody but you.

Mrs. Voluble. For me? well, was ever the like! only see, Betty,
what a Slop Bobby's made! There's no such a thing as having it seen. Come, folks, get up all of you, & let's move
away the Table. Bob, why don't you stir? one would think
you were nailed to your Seat.   340

Bob. Why I'm making all the haste I can, a'n't I?

(*They all rise, & Bob over-turns the Table.*)

Mrs. Voluble. Well, if this is not enough to drive one mad! I
declare I could flee the Boy alive! Here's a Room to see
Company! you great, nasty, stupid Dolt, you, get out of my
Sight this minute.

Bob. Why, mother, I did not do it for the purpose.

Mrs. Voluble. But you did, you great Loggerhead, I know you
did! get out of my sight this minute, I say! (*drives him off
the Stage.*) Well, what's to be done now?— Did ever any
body see such a Room?— I declare I was never in such a   350
pucker in my life. Mrs. Wheedle, do help to put some of
the things into the closet. Look here, if my china Bowl i'n't
broke! I vow I've a great mind to make that looby Eat it for
his Supper.— Betty, why don't you get a mop?— you're as
helpless as a Child.— No, a Broom,— get a Broom, &
sweep them all away at once.— Why you a'n't [8v] going
empty Handed, are you?— I declare you have not half the
Head you was Born with.

Betty. I'm sure I don't know what to do no more than the
Dog. (*gets a Broom.*)   360

Mrs. Voluble. What do you talk so for? have you a mind to
have the Company hear you? (*-The knocking is repeated.-*)
There, they're knocking like mad!— Miss Jenny, what signifies your staring? can't you make yourself a little useful? I'm

---

343 flee: variant of *flay* (OED).

351 pucker: "a state of agitation or excitement; a flutter, a fuss "(*OED*).

353 looby: "A lazy hulking fellow; a lout" (*OED*).

sure if you won't at such a Time as this— why, Betty, why
don't you make haste? Come, poke every thing into the
Closet,— I wonder why Bobby could not have took some
of the things himself,— but as soon as ever he's done the
mischief he thinks of nothing but running away.

(*They clear the stage, & **Miss Jenny** runs to a looking Glass.*)

Miss Jenny. Dear me, what a Figure I've made of myself!   370

Mrs. Voluble. There, now we shall do pretty well. Betty, go &
ask the lady in. (***Exit Betty.***) I declare I'm in such a flustration!

Miss Jenny. So am I, I'm sure, for I'm all of a tremble.

Mrs. Wheedle. Well, if you can spare master Bobby, we'll go
to Mrs. Hollis's directly.

Mrs. Voluble. Spare him? ay, I'm sure it would have been
good luck for me if you had taken him an Hour ago.

Mrs. Wheedle. Well, good by, then. I shall see who the lady
is as I go along.   (***Exit.***)   380

Miss Jenny. It's very unlucky I did not put on my Irish
Muslin. [9r]

Mrs. Voluble. It's prodigious odd what can bring any Company at this Time of night.

Enter **Mrs. Sapient.**

Mrs. Sapient! dear ma'am, I can hardly believe my Eyes!

Mrs. Sapient. I am afraid my visit is unseasonable, but I beg I
may not incommode you.

Mrs. Voluble. Incommode me? dear ma'am no, not the least
in the World; I was doing nothing but just sitting here talking with Miss Jenny, about one thing or another.   390

Mrs. Sapient. I have a question to ask you, Mrs. Voluble,
which—

Mrs. Voluble. I'm sure, ma'am, I shall be very proud to answer it; but if I had but known of the pleasure of seeing
you, I should not have been in such a pickle; but it happened so that we've been a little busy to Day,— you know,
ma'am, in all Families there will be some busy Days,— &
I've the misfortune of a Son, ma'am, who's a little unlucky,

372-73 flustration: a vulgar term for "The condition of being flustered; 'flus-
ter', agitation" (*OED*).

so that puts one a little out of sorts, but he's so unmanage-
able, ma'am, that really—   400

Mrs. Sapient. Well, well, I only want to ask if you know any
thing of Miss Stanley?

Mrs. Voluble. Miss Stanley? to be sure I do, ma'am; why she's
now in my own House here.

Mrs. Sapient. Indeed?— And pray— what, I suppose, she is
[9v]chiefly with Mr. Dabler?—

Mrs. Voluble. No, ma'am, no, she keeps prodigiously snug;
she bid me not tell any body she was here, so I make it a
rule to keep it secret,— unless, indeed, ma'am, to such a
lady as you.   410

Mrs. Sapient. O, it's very safe with me. But, pray, don't you
think Mr. Dabler rather admires her?

Mrs. Voluble. O no, ma'am, not half so much as he admires
another lady of your acquaintance. Ha! Ha!

Mrs. Sapient. Fie, Mrs. Voluble!— but pray, does not he
write a great deal?

Mrs. Voluble. Dear ma'am yes; he's in one continual scribling
from morning to night.

Mrs. Sapient. —Well, &— do you know if he writes about
any particular Person?   420

Mrs. Voluble. O yes, ma'am, he writes about Celia, &
Daphne, & Cleora, &—

Mrs. Sapient. you never see his Poems, do you?

Mrs. Voluble. O dear yes, ma'am, I see them all. why I have
one now in my Pocket about Cleora, that I happened to
pick up this morning. (*aside to* **Miss Jenny.**) Miss Jenny,
do pray put me in mind to put it up before he comes
Home. [*to Mrs. Sapient.*] Should you like to see it,
ma'am?—

Mrs. Sapient. Why— if you have it at Hand—   430

Mrs. Voluble. Dear ma'am, if I had not, I'm sure I'd fetch it,
for I shall be quite proud to oblige you. As to any common
acquaintance, I would not do such a thing upon [10r] any
account, because I should Scorn to do such a baseness to

421–422 Celia, Daphne, & Cleora are conventional names for maidens and
shepherdesses in pastoral poetry; Mrs. Voluble thinks they are real people.

Mr. Dabler, but to such a lady as you it's quite another thing. For, whenever I meet with a lady of Quality, I make it a point to behave in the genteelist manner I can. Perhaps, ma'am, you'd like to see Mr. Dabler's Study?

Mrs. Sapient. O no, not upon any account.

Mrs. Voluble. Because, upon his Table, there's a matter of an hundred of his *miniscrips*.   440

Mrs. Sapient. Indeed?— But when do you expect him Home?

Mrs. Voluble. O not this good while.

Mrs. Sapient. Well then— if you are certain we shall not be surprised—

Mrs. Voluble. O, I'm quite certain of that.

Mrs. Sapient. But, then, for fear of accidents, let your maid order my Coach to wait in the next street.

Mrs. Voluble. Yes, ma'am. Here, Betty!   *(Exit.)*

Mrs. Sapient. This is not quite right, but this Woman would   450
shew them to somebody else if not to me. And now perhaps I may discover whether any of his private Papers contain my name. She will not, for her own sake, dare betray me.

Re-enter Mrs. Voluble.

Mrs. Voluble. Now, ma'am, I'll wait upon you. I assure you, ma'am, I would not do this for every body, only a Lady of your honour I'm sure would be above—

(Exit talking, with Mrs. Sapient,)
Miss Jenny alone.

She's said never a word to *me* all the Time, & I dare [10v] say she knew me as well as could be; but fine ladies Seem to think their Words are made of Gold, they are so afraid of bestowing them.   460

Re-enter Mrs. Voluble.

Mrs. Voluble. O Miss Jenny, only look here! my apron's all stained with the Wine! I never see it till this minute, & now—   **(a knocking at the Door.)**
Oh! *(Screams.)* that's Mr. Dabler's knock! what shall we all do?— run up Stairs & tell the lady this minute,—

(Exit Miss Jenny.)

Betty! Betty! don't go to the Door yet,— I can't think what brings him Home so soon!— here's nothing but ill luck upon ill luck!

Enter **Mrs. Sapient** *with* **Miss Jenny.**

Come, ma'am, come in! Betty!— you may go to the Door
now.   470

Mrs. Sapient. But are you sure he will not come in here?

Mrs. Voluble. O quite, ma'am; he always goes to his own
Room. Hush!— ay, he's gone up,— I heard him pass.

Mrs. Sapient. I am quite surprised, Mrs. Voluble, you should
have deceived me thus; did not you assure me he would
not return this Hour? I must tell you, Mrs. Voluble, that,
whatever you may think of it, *I* shall always regard a Person
who is capable of deceit, to be guilty of insincerity.

Mrs. Voluble. Indeed, ma'am, I knew no more of his return
[11r] than you did, for he makes it a sort of a rule of a 'Sprit   480
night—

Miss Jenny. Ma'am, ma'am, I hear him on the Stairs!

Mrs. Sapient. O hide me,— hide me this Instant anywhere,
—And don't say I am here for the universe!

(*She runs into the closet.*)

Mrs. Voluble. No, ma'am, that I won't if it costs me my
life!— you may always depend upon *me*.   (*shuts her in.*)

Miss Jenny. Laws, what a pickle she'll be in! she's got all
among the broken things.

Enter **Dabler.**

Dabler. Mrs. Voluble, you'll please to make out my account,
for I shall leave your House directly.   490

Mrs. Voluble. Leave my House? Lord, Sir, you quite frighten
me!

Dabler. You have used me very ill, Mrs. Voluble, & curse me
if I shall put up with it!

Mrs. Voluble. Me, Sir? I'm sure, sir, I don't so much as know
what you mean.

Dabler. You have been rummaging all my Papers.

Mrs. Voluble. I?— no, Sir,— I'm sorry, Sir, you suspect me of
such a mean proceeding.

Dabler. 'Tis in vain to deny it; I have often had reason to   500
think it, but now my doubts are confirmed, for my last new
Song, which I called Cleora is no where to be found.

---

501 think] *ins*, suspect *del*

Mrs. Voluble. No where to be found?— you surprise me!— (*aside.*) Good Lank, I quite forgot to put it up! [11v]

Dabler. I'm certain I left it at the top of my Papers.

Mrs. Voluble. Did you indeed, sir? well, I'm sure it's the oddest thing in the World what can be come of it!

Dabler. There is something so gross, so scandalous in this usage, that I am determined not to be duped by it. I shall quit my Lodgings directly;— take your measures accordingly.   510
(*going.*)

Mrs. Voluble. O pray, Sir, Stay,— & if you won't be So angry, I'll tell you the whole truth of the matter.

Dabler. Be quick, then.

Mrs. Voluble, in a low Voice. I'm Sorry, Sir, to betray a lady, but when one's own reputation is at stake—

Dabler. What lady? I don't understand you.

Mrs. Voluble. Hush, hush, Sir!— she'll hear you.

Dabler. She?— Who?

Mrs. Voluble. Why Mrs. Sapient, Sir, (*whispering.*) she's in   520
that closet.

Dabler. What do you mean?

Mrs. Voluble. I'll tell you all, Sir, by & by,— but you must know She came to me, &— &— & begged just to look at your Study, Sir,— So, Sir, never supposing such a lady as that would think of looking at your papers, I was persuaded to agree to it,— but, Sir, as soon as ever we got into the Room, she fell to Reading them without so much as Saying a Word!— while I, all the Time, stood in this manner!— staring with stupification. so, Sir, when you knocked at the   530
Door, she ran down to the closet. [12r]

Dabler. And what has induced her to do all this?

Mrs. Voluble. Ah, Sir, you know well enough! Mrs. Sapient is a Lady of prodigious good Taste; every body knows how she admires Mr. Dabler.

Dabler. Why yes, I don't think she wants Taste.

Mrs. Voluble. Well but, Sir, pray don't stay, for she is quite close crammed in the closet.

Dabler. I think I'll speak to her.

---

519 Who?] ~ .? MS

Mrs. Voluble. Not for the World, Sir! If she knows I've be-   540
trayed her, she'll go beside herself. &, I'm sure, Sir, I would
not have told any body but you upon no account. If you'll
wait up stairs till she's gone, I'll come & tell you all about
it,— but pray, dear Sir, make haste.

Dabler. Yes, She's a good agreeable Woman, & really has a
pretty knowledge of Poetry. Poor Soul!— I begin to be half
Sorry for her.   (*Exit.*)

Mrs. Voluble. I thought he'd never have gone. How do do
now, ma'am?   (*opens the closet Door.*)
                    Enter Mrs. Sapient.

Mrs. Sapient. Crampt to Death! what a strange place have   550
you put me in! Let me begone this Instant,— but are you
sure, Mrs. Voluble, you have not betrayed me?

Mrs. Voluble. I'm surprised, ma'am, you should suspect me! I
would not do such a false thing for never so much, for I always— (*a Knocking at the Door.*) Why now who can that
be?

Mrs. Sapient. How infinitely provoking!— let me go back to
[12v] this frightful closet till the Coast is clear. (*returns to
the Closet.*)

Mrs. Voluble. Well, I think I've managed matters like a
Matchwell.   560
                    Enter Mrs. Wheedle.

Mrs. Wheedle. O, I'm quite out of Breath,— I never walked
so fast in my life.

Mrs. Voluble. Where have you left Bobby?

Mrs. Wheedle. He's gone into the Kitchen. I must see Miss
Stanley directly.

Mrs. Voluble. We've been in perilous danger since you went.
Do you know (*in a low Voice,*) Mrs. Sapient is now in the
Closet? Be sure you don't tell any body.

Mrs. Wheedle. No, not for the World. Miss Jenny pray step &
tell Miss Stanley I'm come back.   (*Exit Miss Jenny.*)   570

557-558 back to / this frightful] back to [*catchword* this] / frightful *MS*
560 *Matchwell*] *lc MS*
560 *Matchwell*: apparently a matchmaker; possibly a character in a comedy
seen by Burney, but no source discovered.

Mrs. Voluble. Well, & while you speak to her, I'll go & talk over Mr. Dabler, & contrive to poke this nasty Song under the Table. But first I'll say something to the poor lady in the closet. Ma'am! (*opens the Door.*) if you've a mind to keep Still, you'll hear all what Miss Stanley says presently, for she's coming down.

Mrs. Sapient. Are you mad, Mrs. Voluble?— what do you hold the Door open for?— Would you have that Woman see me?

Mrs. Voluble. Ma'am, I beg your pardon! (*shuts the Door.*) I   580
won't help her out this half Hour for that crossness.

(*Exit.*)

Mrs. Wheedle. These fine Ladies go through any thing for the sake of curiosity.

Enter Cecilia

Cecilia. Well, Mrs. Wheedle, have you seen Mrs. Hollis? [13r]

Mrs. Wheedle. Yes, ma'am, & she's quite agreeable to your proposal: but as she's going very soon, & will be glad to be fixed, She says she shall take it as a particular favour if you will go to her House to night.

Cecilia. Impossible! I must consult some friend ere I go at all.

Mrs. Wheedle. But, ma'am, she begs you will, for she says   590
she's heard of your misfortunes, & shall be glad to give you her advice what to do.

Cecilia. Then I *will* go to her!— for never yet did poor Creature more want advice & assistance!

Mrs. Wheedle. Betty! (*calls at the Door.*) go & get a Coach. I'll [just] go speak to Mrs. Voluble ma'am, & come again

(*Exit.*)

Cecilia alone.

Perhaps I may repent this Enterprize,— my Heart fails me already;— & yet, how few are those human actions that repentance may not pursue! Error precedes almost every step, & sorrow follows every error. I who to happiness   600
have bid a long, a last farewell, must content myself with seeking Peace in retirement & Solitude, & endeavour to

---

580 (*shuts the Door.*)] shuts the Door. *MS*
596 I ~ (*Exit.*)] *ins*, Cecilia. Perhaps I may repent this Enter *del*
599 precedes] *ins* follows *del*

contract all my wishes to preserving my own Innocence
from the contagion of this bad & most deseased World's
corruptions.

Enter Betty.

Betty. Ma'am the Coach is at the Door.

Cecilia. Alas! [13v]

Betty. Mrs. Wheedle, ma'am, is gone up stairs to my *Mississ*,
but she says she'll be ready in a few minutes.   (*Exit.*)

Cecilia alone.

Oh cease, fond, suffering, feeble Heart! to struggle thus   610
with misery inevitable. Beaufort is no longer the Beaufort
he appeared, & since he has lost even the semblance of his
Worth, why should this sharp regret pursue his Image? But,
alas, that semblance which *he* has lost, *I* must ever retain!
fresh, fair & perfect it is still before me!— Oh why must
Woe weaken all faculties but the memory?— I will reason
no longer,— I will think of him no more,— I will offer myself to servitude, for Labour itself must be less insupportable than this gloomy indolence of sorrowing reflection—
where is this Woman?—   (*going.*)   620

Enter Beaufort, who stops her.

Beaufort. My Cecilia!—

Cecilia. Oh — good Heaven!

Beaufort. My lov'd, lost, injured,— my adored Cecilia!

Cecilia. Am I awake?

Beaufort. Whence this surprise?— my love, my Heart's sweet
Partner—

Cecilia. Oh forbear!— these terms are no longer— Mr. Beaufort, let me pass!

Beaufort. What do I hear?

Cecilia. Leave me, sir,— I cannot talk with you,— leave [14r]   630
me, I say!

Beaufort. Leave you?— (*offering to take her Hand.*)

Cecilia. Yes,— (*turning from him,*) for I cannot bear to look
at you!

Beaufort. Not look at me? what have I done? how have I offended you? why are you thus dreadfully changed?

Cecilia. *I* changed? comes this well from *you*?— but I will not

recriminate, niether will I converse with you any longer.
You see me now perhaps for the last Time,— I am prepar-
ing to quit the Kingdom.   640
Beaufort. To quit the Kingdom?
Cecilia. Yes; it is a Step which your own conduct has com-
pelled me to take.
Beaufort. My Conduct?— who has belied me to you?— what
villain—
Cecilia. No one, Sir; you have done your work yourself.
Beaufort. Cecilia, do you mean to distract me?— if not, explain, & instantly, your dark, your cruel meaning.
Cecilia. Can it want explanation to *you*? have you Shocked
me in ignorance, & irritated me without knowing it? [14v]   650
Beaufort. I shocked?— I irritated you?—
Cecilia. Did you not, in the very first anguish of a calamity
which you alone had the power to alleviate neglect & avoid
me? Send me a cold message by a Friend? Suffer me to endure indignities without support, & Sorrows without participation? Leave me, defenceless, to be crushed by impend-
ing ruin? & abandon my aching Heart to all the torture of
new-born fears, unprotected, unassured, & uncomforted?
Beaufort. Can *I* have done all this?
Cecilia. I know not,— but I am sure it has seem'd so.   660
Beaufort. Oh wretched policy of cold, unfeeling Prudence,
had I listened to no dictates but those of my Heart, I had
never been wounded with suspicions & reproaches so
cruel.
Cecilia. Rather say, had your Heart sooner known it's own
docility, you might have permitted Lady Smatter to dispose
of it ere the deluded Cecilia was known to you.
Beaufort. Barbarous Cecilia! take not such a Time as this to
depreciate my Heart in your opinion, for now— 'tis all I
have to offer you.   670
Cecilia. You know too well— 'tis all I ever valued. [15r]
Beaufort. Oh take it then,— receive it once more, & with
that confidence in it's Faith which it never deserved to for-
feit! Painfully I submitted to advice I abhorred, but though
my Judgement has been overpowered, my truth has been

inviolate. Turn not from me, Cecilia!— if I have tempo-
rized, it has been less for my own Sake than for yours; but I
have seen the vanity of my expectations,— I have dis-
obeyed Lady Smatter,— I have set all consequences at defiance, & flown in the very face of ruin,— & now, will *you*,   680
Cecilia, (*Kneeling*) reject, disdain & Spurn me?

Cecilia. Oh Beaufort— is it possible I can have wronged you?

Beaufort. Never, my sweetest Cecilia, if now you pardon me.

Cecilia. Pardon you?— too generous Beaufort— ah! rise.

            Enter Lady Smatter & Mr. Codger.

Beaufort, *rising.* Lady Smatter!

Lady Smatter. How, Beaufort here?— & kneeling, too!

Codger. Son Beaufort, I cannot deny but I think it is rather an
extraordinary thing that you should chuse to be seen Kneeling to that young lady, knowing, I presume, that your Aunt
Smatter disaffects your [15v] so doing.   690

Lady Smatter. Beaufort, I see you are resolved to keep no
terms with me. As to Miss Stanley, I renounce her with contempt; I came hither with the most generous views of as-
sisting her, & prevailed with Mr. Codger to conduct her to
her Friends in the country; but since I find her capable of
so much baseness, since I see that all her little arts are at
Work—

Cecilia. Forbear, madam, these unmerited reproaches; believe me, I will niether become a Burthen to you, nor a
Scorn to myself; the measures I have taken I doubt not will   700
meet with your Ladyship's approbation, though it is by no
means incumbent upon me, thus contemptuously accused,
to enter into any defence or explanation.   (*Exit.*)

Beaufort. Stay, my Cecilia,— hear me—   (*follows her.*)

Lady Smatter. How? persue her in defiance of my presence?
Had I a Pen & Ink I should disinherit him incontinently.
Who are all these People?

        Enter Miss Jenny, Mrs Voluble, & Mrs. Wheedle.

Miss Jenny *as she Enters.* Law, only look! here's Lady Smatter & an Old Gentleman!

---

676 Cecilia] *cor, lc or*
706 incontinently: "straightaway, at once, immediately" (*OED*).

Mrs. Voluble. What, in my Parlour? well, I declare, & so there   710
is! why how could they get in?

Mrs. Wheedle. I suppose the Door's open because of the
[16r] Hackney Coach. But as to Miss Stanley, I believe she's
hid herself.

Codger. Madam, I can give your Ladyship no Satisfaction.

Lady Smatter. About what?

Codger. About these people, madam, that your Ladyship was
enquiring after, for, to the best of my knowledge, madam, I
apprehend I never saw any of them before.

Lady Smatter. I see who they are myself, now.   720

Mrs. Voluble, advancing to Lady Smatter. My Lady, I hope
your Ladyship's well; I am very glad, my lady, to pay my
humble duty to your Ladyship in my poor House, & I
hope—

Lady Smatter. Pray is Mr. Dabler at Home?

Mrs. Voluble. Yes, my lady, & indeed—

Lady Smatter. Tell him, then, I shall be glad to see him.

Mrs. Voluble. Yes, my lady. [*aside to Miss Jenny.*] I suppose, Miss Jenny, you little thought of my having such a
genteel acquaintance among the Quality!   [*Exit.*]   730

Miss Jenny aside to Mrs. Wheedle. I'm afraid that poor lady
in the Closet will spoil all her things.

Lady Smatter. Yes, I'll consult with Mr. Dabler; for as to this
old Soul, it takes him half an Hour to recollect whether 2 &
3 make 5 or 6.

Enter Censor.

Censor. I have, with some difficulty, traced your Ladyship
hither.

Lady Smatter. Then, Sir, you have traced me to a most delightful spot; & you will find your Friend as [16v] self-
willed, refractory & opinionated as your amplest instruc-   740
tions can have rendered him.

Censor. I would advise your Ladyship to think a little less for
Him, & a little more for yourself, lest in your solicitude for
his Fortune, you lose all care for your own Fame.

728–730 lady. [*aside* ~ Quality! [*Exit.*]] lady. I ~ Quality! *Aside to Miss
Jenny & Exit MS*

730 Quality] *cor, original word indecipherable*

Lady Smatter. My Fame? I don't understand you.

Censor. Nay, if you think such Lampoons may spread without doing you injury—

Lady Smatter. Lampoons? What Lampoons?— sure nobody has dared—

Enter Dabler & Mrs. Voluble.

Mrs. Voluble. Why here's Mr. Censor too! I believe there'll   750
be Company coming in all night.

Lady Smatter. Mr. Censor, I say, if there is any Lampoon that concerns *me*, I insist upon hearing it directly.

Censor. I picked it up just now at a Coffee House.
(*reads.*) Yes, Smatter is the Muse's Friend,
            She knows to censure or commend;
            And has of Faith & Truth such store
            She'll ne'er desert you— till you're poor.

Lady Smatter. What insolent impertinence!

Dabler. Poor Stuff! poor Stuff indeed! your Ladyship should   760
regard these little Squibs as *I* do, mere impotent efforts of Envy.

Lady Smatter. O I do; I'd rather hear them than not.

Dabler. And ill done, too; most contemptibly ill done. I [17r] think I'll answer it for your Ladyship.

Censor. Hark ye, Mr. Dabler, (*takes him aside*) do you know this Paper?

Dabler. That Paper?

Censor. Yes, Sir; it contains the lines which you passed off at Lady Smatter's as made at the moment.   770

Dabler. Why, Sir, that was merely— it happened—

Censor. It is too late for equivocation, Sir; your reputation is now wholly in my power, & I can instantly blast it, alike with respect to Poetry & to Veracity.

Dabler. Surely, Sir—

Censor. If, therefore, you do not, with your utmost skill, assist me to reconcile Lady Smatter to her Nephew & his choice, I will shew this original Copy of your extemporary abilities to every body who will take the trouble to read it:

766 (*takes him aside*)] takes him aside *MS*
769 passed off] passed of *MS*

otherwise, I will sink the whole transaction, & return you   780
this glaring proof of it.

Dabler. To be sure, Sir,— as to Mr. Beaufort's choice— it's
the thing in the World I most approve,— & so—

Censor. Well, Sir, you know the alternative, & must act as you
please.

Dabler. (*aside.*) What cursed ill luck!

Lady Smatter. Mr. Censor, I more than half suspect you are
yourself the author of that pretty Lampoon.

Censor. Nay, madam, you see this is not my Writing.

Lady Smatter. Give it me.   790

Censor. Hold,— here's something on the other side which I
did not see. [17v]

(*reads.*) Were madness stinted to Moorfields
    The World elsewhere would be much thinner;
        To Time now Smatter's Beauty yields—

Lady Smatter. How!

Censor reading. She fain in Wit would be a Winner.
        At Thirty she began to read,—

Lady Smatter. That's false!— entirely false!

Censor, reads. At Forty, it is said, could spell,—   800

Lady Smatter. How's that? at Forty?— Sir this is your own
putting in.

Censor, reads. At Fifty—

Lady Smatter. At Fifty?— ha! ha! ha!— this is droll enough!

Censor, reads. At Fifty, 'twas by all agreed
    A common School Girl she'd excell.

Lady Smatter. What impertinent nonsense!

Censor, reads. Such wonders did the World presage—

Lady Smatter. Mr. Censor, I desire you'll read no more,— 'tis
such rubbish it makes me quite Sick.   810

Censor, reads. Such wonders did the World presage
    From Blossoms which such Fruit invited,—
        When Avarice,— the vice of Age,—
    Stept in,— & all expectance blighted.

Lady Smatter. Of Age!— I protest this is the most impudent
thing I ever heard in my life! calculated for no purpose in
the World but to insinuate I am growing old. [18r]

Censor. You have certainly some secret Enemy, who avails

himself of your disagreement with Miss Stanley to prejudice
the World against you.   820

Lady Smatter. O, I'm certain I can tell who it is.

Censor. Who?

Lady Smatter. Mrs. Sapient.

Miss Jenny. (*aside.*) Law, I'm afraid she'll hear them.

Lady Smatter. Not that I suspect her of the Writing, for mis-
erable Stuff as it is, I know her capacity is yet below it; but
she was the first to leave my House when the affair was discovered, & I suppose She has been tatling it about the
Town ever since.

Mrs. Voluble. (*aside.*) Ah, poor lady, it's all to fall upon her!   830

Censor. Depend upon it, madam, this will never rest here;
your Ladyship is so well known, that one satire will but be
the prelude to another.

Lady Smatter. Alas, how dangerous is popularity! O Mr.
Dabler, that I could but despise these libels as you do!—
but this last is insufferable,— yet you, I suppose, would
think it nothing?

Dabler. No, really, ma'am, I can't say that,— no, not as *nothing,*— that is, not absolutely as nothing,— for— for libels
of this sort— are rather—   840

Lady Smatter. How? I thought you held them all in contempt?

Dabler. So I do, ma'am, only—

Censor. You do, Sir?—

Dabler. No, Sir, no; I don't mean to absolutely say that,— that
is, only in regard to *myself,*— for we men do not [18v] suffer in the World by Lampoons as the poor Ladies do;—
they, indeed, may be quite— quite ruined by them.

Lady Smatter. Nay, Mr. Dabler, now *you* begin to distress
me.   850

Enter Jack, Singing.

She has ta'en such a Dose of incongruous matter
That Bedlam must Soon hold the Carcase of Smatter

Lady Smatter. How?— what?— the Carcase of Who?—

Jack. Ha! Ha! Ha! faith, madam, I beg your pardon, but who'd
have thought of meeting your Ladyship here?— O Dabler, I
have such a thing to tell you! (*whispers him & Laughs.*)

Lady Smatter. I shall go mad!— What were you Singing, Jack,— what is it you Laugh at?— why won't you Speak?

Jack. I'm so much hurried I can't stay to answer your Lady-ship now. Dabler, be sure Keep counsel. Ha! Ha! Ha,— I must go & Sing it to Billy Skip & Will. Scamper, or I sha'n't Sleep a Wink all night.   (*going.*)   860

Lady Smatter. This is intolerable! Stay, Jack, I charge you! Mr. Codger, how unmoved you stand! Why don't you make him stay?

Codger. Madam I will. Son Jack, Stay.

Jack. Lord, Sir,—

Lady Smatter. I am half Choaked!— Mr. Codger you would provoke a Saint! why don't you make him tell you what he was Singing?   870

Codger. Madam he is so giddy Pated he never understands me. Son Jack, you attend to nothing! Don't you perceive that her Ladyship seems curious to know what [19r] Song you were humming?

Jack. Why, Sir, it was only a new Ballad.

Lady Smatter. A Ballad with *my* name in it? Explain yourself instantly!

Jack. Here it is,— shall I Sing it or Say it?

Lady Smatter. You shall do niether,— give it me!

Censor. No, no, Sing it first for the good of the Company.   880

Jack. Your Ladyship won't take it ill?

Lady Smatter. Ask me no Questions,— I don't know what I shall do.

Jack, Sings. I call not to Swains to attend to my Song;
        Nor call I to Damsels, so tender & young;
        To Critics, & Pedants, & Doctors I clatter,
        For who else will heed what becomes of poor Smatter.
            with a down, down, derry down.

Lady Smatter. How? is my name at full length?

Jack, sings. This lady with Study has muddled her head;   890
        Sans meaning she talk'd, & Sans knowledge she read,
        And gulp'd such a Dose of incongruous matter
        That Bedlam must soon hold the Carcase of Smatter.
            with a down, down, derry down.

Lady Smatter. The Carcase of Smatter?— it can't be,— no
one would dare—

Jack. Ma'am if you stop me so often, I shall be too late to go
& Sing it any where else to night. (*Sings.*)

    She thought Wealth esteeme'd by the foolish alone, [19v]

    So, shunning offence, never offer'd her own;   900

    And when her Young Friend dire misfortune did batter,

    Too Wise to relieve her was kind Lady Smatter.

       with a down, down, derry down.

Lady Smatter. I'll hear no more! (*walks about in disorder.*)

Censor. Sing on, however, Jack; we'll hear it out.

Jack, Sings. Her Nephew she never corrupted with pelf,

    Holding Starving a Virtue— for all but herself

    Of Gold was Her Goblet, of Silver, Her platter,

    To shew how such Ore was degraded by Smatter.

       with a down, down, derry down.   910

    A Club she supported of Witlings & Fools,

    Who, but for her Dinners, had scoff'd at her rules;

    The reason, if any she had, these did shatter

    Of poor empty-Headed, & little-Soul'd Smatter.

       with a down, down, derry down.

Lady Smatter. Empty-Headed?— little Souled?— who has
dared write this?— Where did you get it?

Jack. From a man who was carrying it to the Printers.

Lady Smatter. To the Printers?— O insupportable!— are they
going to Print it?— Mr. Dabler why don't you assist me?—   920
how can I have it suppressed?— Speak quick, or I shall die.

Dabler. Really, ma'am, I— I—

Censor. There is but one way,— make a Friend of the Writer.

Lady Smatter. I detest him from my Soul,— & I believe 'tis
yourself!

Censor. Your Ladyship is not deceived;— I have the honour
to be the [20r] identical Person. (*Bowing.*)

Lady Smatter. Nay, then, I see your drift,— but depend upon
it, I will not be Duped by you.   (*going.*)

Censor. Hear me, madam!—   930

Lady Smatter. No, not a Word!

---

906 pelf: wealth—particularly that which is dishonestly accumulated (*OED*).

Censor. You must! (*holds the Door.*) You have but one moment for reflection, either to establish your Fame upon the
firmest foundation, or to consign yourself for life to Irony &
Contempt.

Lady Smatter. I will have you prosecuted with the utmost
severity of the Law.

Censor. You will have the thanks of my Printer for your reward.

Lady Smatter. You will not dare—

Censor. I dare do any thing to repel the injuries of Inno-   940
cence! I have already shewn you my *power*, & you will
find my *Courage* undaunted, & my *perseverance* indefatigable. If you any longer oppose the union of your Nephew
with Miss Stanley, I will destroy the whole peace of your
Life.

Lady Smatter. You cannot!— I defy you!   (*walks from him.*)

Censor. I will drop Lampoons in every Coffee-House,—

                                          (*following her.*)

Lady Smatter. You are welcome, Sir.—

Censor. Compose Daily Epigrams for all the Papers,—

Lady Smatter. With all my Heart,—   950

Censor. Send libels to every corner of the Town,—

Lady Smatter. I care not!—

Censor. Make all the Ballad Singers resound your Deeds,

Lady Smatter. You cannot!— *shall* not!

Censor. And treat the Patagonian Theatre with a Poppet to
represent you. [20v]

Lady Smatter bursting into Tears. This is too much to be
borne, Mr. Censor, you are a Daemon!

Censor. But, if you relent,— I will burn all I have written, &
forget all I have planned; Lampoons shall give place to pan-   960
egyric, & libels, to Songs of Triumph; the liberality of your
Soul, & the depth of your knowledge shall be recorded by
the Muses, & echoed by the whole Nation!

---

932 (*holds the Door.*)] holds the Door. *MS*
955 Patagonian Theatre: A puppet ("poppet") theatre patronized by London's fashionable society; it operated from 1776 to 1781 (George Speight,
The History of the English Puppet Theatre [New York: J. de Graff, 1955],
117–124).

Lady Smatter. I am half distracted!— Mr. Dabler, why don't you counsel me?— how cruel is your Silence!

Dabler. Why, certainly, ma'am, what— what Mr Censor says—

Censor. Speak out, man!— Tell Lady Smatter if she will not be a lost Woman to the Literary World, should she, in this trial of her magnanimity, disgrace it's expectations? Speak boldly!   970

Dabler. Hem!— you,— you have Said, Sir,— just what I think.

Lady Smatter. How? are *you* against me?— nay then—

Censor. Every body must be against you; even Mr. Codger, as I can discern by his looks. Are you not, Sir?

Codger. Sir, I can by no means decide upon so important a Question, without maturely pondering upon the several pre-liminaries.

Censor. Come, madam, consider what is expected from the celebrity of your character,— consider the applause that awaits you in the World;— you will be another Sacharissa, a Second Sapho,— a tenth muse.   980

Lady Smatter. I know not what to do!— allow me, at least, a few Days for meditation, & forbear these scandalous libels till—

Censor. No, madam, not an Hour!— there is no Time so ill spent as that which is passed in deliberating between [21r] meanness & Generosity! You may now not only gain the es-teem of the Living, but— if it is not Mr. Dabler's fault,— consign your name with Honour to Posterity.   990

Lady Smatter. To Posterity?— why where is this Girl gone?— what has Beaufort done with himself?—

Censor. Now, madam, you have Bound me yours for-ever!— here, Beaufort!— Miss Stanley!—   *(goes out.)*

Jack. Huzza!—

Codger. Madam, to confess the verity, I must acknowledge

---

981 awaits] *cor*, waits *or*
981-982 Sacharissa is the name Edmund Waller (1606-1687) gave to the Lady Dorothea Sidney when he courted her in verse. Sappho was an ancient Greek woman poet (620-565 B.C.). The Muses were the nine female spirits presiding over art, music and poetry.
995 Jack] *cor*, Cod *or*

that I do not rightly comprehend what it is your Ladyship has determined upon doing?

Lady Smatter. No; nor would you, were I to take an Hour to tell you. 1000

Re-enter Censor, with Beaufort & Cecilia.

Beaufort. O madam, is it indeed true that—

Lady Smatter. Beaufort, I am so much flurried, I hardly know what is true;— save, indeed, that Pity, as a certain author says, will ever, in noble minds, conquer Prudence. Miss Stanley—

Censor. Come, come, no speeches; this whole Company bears Witness to your Consent to their marriage, & your Ladyship *(in a low voice.)* may depend upon not losing sight of *me* till the Ceremony is over.

Cecilia. Lady Smatter's returning favour will once more de- 1010 vote me to her Service; but I am happy to find, by this Letter, that my affairs are in a less desperate situation than I had apprehended. *(gives a Letter to Lady Smatter.)* But here, Mr. Censor, is another Letter which I do not quite so well understand; it contains an order for £5000, & is signed with your name?

Censor. Pho, pho, we will talk of that another Time. [21v]

Cecilia. Impossible! Liberality so undeserved—

Censor. Not a Word more, I entreat you!

Cecilia. Indeed I can never accept it. 1020

Censor. Part with it as you can! *I* have got rid of it. I merit no thanks, for I mean it not in Service to you, but in Spite to Lady Smatter, that she may not have the pleasure of boasting, to her wondering Witlings, that she received a Niece wholly unportioned. Beaufort, but for his own Stubbornness, had long since possessed it,— from a similar motive.

Cecilia. Dwells Benevolence in so rugged a Garb?— Oh Mr. Censor—!

Beaufort. Noble, generous Censor! you penetrate my Heart,— yet I cannot consent— 1030

Censor. Pho, pho, never praise a man for only gratifying his own humour.

Enter Bob, running.

Bob. Mother, mother, I believe there's a Cat in the closet!

Mrs. Voluble. Hold your Tongue, you great oaf!

Bob. Why, mother, as I was in the Back Parlour, you can't think what a rustling it made.

Miss Jenny. (*aside.*) Dear me!— it's the poor lady!—

Mrs. Wheedle. Well, what a thing is this!

Mrs. Voluble. Bob, I could beat your Brains out!

Bob. Why Lord, mother, where's the great harm of saying   1040
there's a Cat in the closet?

Jack. The best way is to look.   (*goes toward the closet.*)

Dabler. Not for the World! I won't suffer it!

Jack. You won't Suffer it?— Pray, Sir, does the Cat belong to
you? [22r]

Bob. Mother, I dare say she's Eating up all the Victuals.

Jack. Come then, my Lad, you & I'll Hunt her.

(*brushes past Dabler, & opens the Door.*)

All.} Mrs. Sapient!

Mrs. Sapient, coming forward. Sir, this impertinent curiosity—

Jack. Lord, ma'am, I beg your pardon! I'm sure I would not   1050
have opened the Door for the World, only we took you for
the Cat. If you please, ma'am, I'll shut you in again.

Lady Smatter. That's a pretty snug retreat you have chosen,
Mrs. Sapient.

Censor. To which of the Muses, madam, may that Temple be
Dedicated?

Jack. I hope, ma'am, you made use of your Time to mend
your furbelows?

Codger. Madam, as I don't understand this quick way of
Speaking, I should be much obliged if you would take the   1060
trouble to make plain to my comprehension the reason of
your chusing to be shut up in that dark closet?

1048 This concealment scene is perhaps too derivative of the famous screen
scene in the fourth act of *The School for Scandal* by Richard Brinsley Sheridan (1751-1816). The play was originally performed in 1777; according to
The London Stage, it was subsequently performed every season through the
end of the century. Sheridan, who was owner of the Drury Lane theatre (as
well as Burney's most likely producer), might perhaps have suggested revi-
sion, as his own scene would be fresh in the minds of the audience.

Censor. Doubtless, Sir, for the Study of the Occult Sciences.

Lady Smatter. Give me leave, madam, to recommend to your perusal this passage of Addison; Those who conceal themselves to hear the Counsels of others, commonly have little reason to be satisfied with what they hear of themselves.

Mrs. Sapient. And give *me* leave, ma'am, to observe,— though I pretend not to assert it positively,— that, in *my* opinion, those who speak ill of people in their absence,   1070 give no great proof of a Sincere Friendship.

Censor. (*aside.*) I begin to hope these **Witlings** will demolish their Club. [22v]

Dabler. (*aside.*) Faith, if they Quarrel, I'll not Speak till they part.

Beaufort. Allow me, Ladies, with all humility, to mediate, & to entreat that the calm of an Evening succeeding a Day So agitated with Storms, may be enjoyed without allay. Terror, my Cecilia, now ceases to alarm, & Sorrow, to oppress us; gratefully let us receive returning Happiness, & hope that our Ex-   1080 ample,— should any attend to it,— may inculcate this most useful of all practical precepts: That Self-dependance is the first of Earthly Blessings; since those who rely solely on others for support & protection are not only liable to the common vicissitudes of Human Life, but exposed to the partial   1085 caprices & infirmities of Human Nature.

Finis.

1065-1067 "Those who conceal themselves. . . ." Addison's *Spectator* no. 439 (1712) deals with Reputation and Fame, and discusses the vulgarity of those who contrive to eavesdrop in the hopes of hearing something of themselves (4: 42-45). Lady Smatter is correct in attributing the sentiment to Addison, but her proclamation is neither a direct quotation nor a close paraphrase of his text.

1082 precepts: That] precepts That *MS*

SELECTED BIBLIOGRAPHY

Primary Sources

A Busy Day. Ed. Tara Ghoshal Wallace. New Brunswick: Rutgers University Press, 1984.

Camilla: or A Picture of Youth. 1796. Eds. Edward A. Bloom and Lillian D. Bloom. New York: Oxford University Press, 1982.

Cecilia; or, Memoirs of an Heiress. 1782. Eds. Peter Sabor and Margaret Doody. Oxford: Oxford University Press, 1988.

The Diary and Letters of Madame d'Arblay, 1778-1840. Ed. Charlotte Barrett. 7 vols. London: Henry Colburn, 1842-1846. Ed. Austin Dobson. 6 vols. London: Macmillan, 1904-1905.

The Early Diary of Frances Burney, 1768-78. Ed. Annie Raine Ellis. 2 vols. London: Bell, 1907.

The Early Journals and Letters of Fanny Burney. vols 1 and 2. Ed. Lars E. Troide. Toronto: University of Toronto Press, 1988-1991.

Edwy and Elgiva. Ed. Miriam J. Benkovitz. Hamden: The Shoe String Press, 1957.

Evelina; or, The History of a Young Lady's Entrance into the World. 1778. Ed. Edward A. Bloom. Oxford: Oxford University Press, 1982.

The Journals and Letters of Fanny Burney (Madame d'Arblay). Ed. Joyce Hemlow, et. al. 10 vols. Oxford: Clarendon, 1972-82

Memoirs of Dr. Burney. 3 vols. 1832. rpt. New York: AMS Press, 1975.

The Wanderer; or, Female Difficulties. 1814. Eds. Margaret Anne Doody, Robert L. Mack and Peter Sabor. Oxford: Oxford University Press, 1990.

Manuscripts of plays unpublished during Burney's lifetime, now in the Berg Collection of the New York Public Library.

"The Witlings" 1778-1779

"Edwy and Elgiva" 1790-1791

"Elberta" 1790-1791

"Hubert De Vere" 1790-1791

"The Siege of Pevensy" 1790-1791

"A Busy Day" 1800-1801

"Love and Fashion" 1798-1799

"The Woman Hater" 1800-1801

Secondary Sources

Addison, Joseph, Richard Steele, et al. *The Spectator*. Ed. Donald F. Bond. 5 vols. Oxford: Clarendon, 1965.

Adelstein, Michael E. *Fanny Burney*. New York: Twayne Publishers, 1968.

Bayne-Powell, Rosamond. *Eighteenth-Century London Life*. New York: E.P. Dutton, 1938.

Bernbaum, Ernest. *The Drama of Sensibility*. Boston: Ginn, 1915.

Bloom, Lillian D., and Edward A. Bloom. "Fanny Burney's Novels: The Retreat From Wonder." *Novel* 12 (1979): 215-35.

Bodek, Evelyn Gordon. "Salonieres and Bluestockings: Educated Obsolesence and Germinating Feminism." *Feminist Studies* 3 (Spring-Summer 1976): 185-199.

Boswell, James. *Life of Johnson, Including Boswell's Journey of a Tour to the Hebrides and Johnson's Diary of a Journey into North Wales*. Ed. George Birkbeck Hill. 6 vols. Oxford: Clarendon, 1887.

Brown, Martha. "Fanny Burney's 'Feminism': Gender or Genre?" *Fetter'd or Free: Women Novelists 1670-1815*. Eds. Mary Anne Schofield and Cecilia Macheski. Athens: Ohio University Press, 1986.

Busse, John. *Mrs. Montagu: Queen of the Blues*. London: Gerald Howe, 1928.

Clifford, James L. *Hester Lynch Piozzi (Mrs. Thrale)*. 2nd. edition. Oxford: Clarendon, 1952.

Crosland, Mrs. Newton. "Madame d'Arblay and Mrs. Piozzi." *Memorable Women: The Story of Their Lives*. Boston: Ticknor and Fields, 1854.

Cutting, Rose Marie. "Defiant Women: The Growth of Feminism in Fanny Burney's Novels." *Studies in English Literature* 17 (1977): 519-530.

Dobson, Austin. Preface and Notes. *The Diary and Letters of Madame D'Arblay, As Edited By Her Niece, Charlotte Barrett*. 6 vols. New York: Macmillan, 1905.

_____. Fanny Burney. New York: Macmillan, 1903.

Doody, Margaret. *Frances Burney: The Life In The Works*. New Brunswick, N.J.: Rutgers University Press, 1988.

Doran, John. *A Lady of the Last Century (Mrs. Elizabeth Montagu)*. London: Bentley & Son, 1873.

George, M. Dorothy. *London Life in the Eighteenth Century*. New York: Harper & Row, 1964.

Grau, Joseph A. *Fanny Burney: An Annotated Bibliography*. New York: Garland Publishing, 1981.

Hemlow, Joyce, ed. *A Catalogue of the Burney Family Correspondence, 1749-1878*. New York: The New York Public Library, 1971.

_____. "Fanny Burney and the Courtesy Books." *PMLA* 65 (1950): 732-61.

_____. "Fanny Burney: Playwright." *University of Toronto Quarterly* 19 (1950): 170-89.

_____. *The History of Fanny Burney*. Oxford: Clarendon, 1958.

_____. "Letters and Journals of Fanny Burney: Establishing the Text." *Editing Eighteenth-Century Texts*. Toronto: University of Toronto Press, 1968., 25-43.

Hill, Constance. *Fanny Burney at the Court of Queen Charlotte*. London: John Lane, 1907.

_____. *The House in St. Martin's St.* London: John Lane, 1907.

Howard-Hill, T.H. "Playwrights' Intentions and the Editing of Plays." *TEXT* 4 (1988): 263-272.

Huchon, R. *Mrs. Montagu and Her Friends*. London: John Murray, 1907.

Hume, Robert D. ed. *The London Theatre World, 1660-1800*. Carbondale: Southern Illinois University Press, 1980.

_____. *The Rakish Stage: Studies in English Drama*, 1660-1800. Carbondale: Southern Illinois University Press, 1983.

Johnson, Samuel. *A Dictionary of the English Language* (1755). rpt. New York: AMS Press, 1967.

_____. *The Yale Edition of the Works of Samuel Johnson*. 9 vols. Gen. ed. Allen T. Hazen. New Haven: Yale University Press, 1958-1971.

Kowaleski-Wallace, Beth. "Milton's Daughters: The Education of Eighteenth Century Women Writers." *Feminist Studies* 12 (1986): 275-293.

Leranbaum, Miriam. "Mistresses of Orthodoxy: Education in the Lives and Writings of Late Eighteenth-Century Women Writers." *Proceedings of the American Philosophical Society* 121 (1977): 281-301.

Lobban, J. H. "The Blue-Stockings." *Blackwood's Magazine* 180 (October 1906): 452-469.

The London Stage 1660-1800. 5 pts, 15 vols. Eds. William Van Lennep, et al. Carbondale: Southern Illinois University Press, 1960-1968.

Lynch, James J. *Box Pit and Gallery: Stage and Society in Johnson's London*. New York: Russell and Russell, 1971.

Macaulay, Thomas Babington. "Madame d'Arblay." *Edinburgh Review* 76 (January 1843): 523–70.

McCarthy, William. *Hester Thrale Piozzi: Portrait of a Literary Woman*. Chapel Hill: University of North Carolina Press, 1985.

Moers, Ellen. *Literary Women*. New York: Oxford University Press, 1976.

Montagu, Elizabeth Robinson. *The Letters of Mrs. Elizabeth Montagu With Some of the Letters of her Correspondents*. London: T. Cadell and W. Davies, 1809–13.

_____. *Mrs. Montagu, 'Queen of the Blues': Her Letters and Friendships from 1720–1761*. 2 vols. Ed. Emily J. Climenson. New York: E. P. Dutton, 1906.

_____. *Mrs. Montagu, 'Queen of the Blues': Her Letters and Friendships from 1762 to 1800*. 2 vols. Ed. Reginald Blunt. Boston and New York: Houghton Mifflin Company, 1923.

Morrison, Marjorie Lee. "Fanny Burney and the Theatre." Unpublished Doctoral Dissertation. Austin: University of Texas, 1957.

Mulliken, Elizabeth Yost. "The Influence of the Drama on Fanny Burney's Novels." Unpublished Doctoral Dissertation. Madison: University of Wisconsin, 1969.

Nicoll, Allardyce. *The Garrick Stage: Theatres and Audience in the Eighteenth Century*. Manchester: Manchester University Press, 1980.

_____. *A History of Late Eighteenth Century Drama: 1750–1800*. Cambridge: Cambridge University Press, 1937.

Pedicord, Harry William. *The Theatrical Public in the Time of Garrick*. Carbondale: Southern Illinois University Press, 1954.

Rogers, Katharine C., "Fanny Burney: The Private Self and the Published Self." *International Journal of Women's Studies* 7 (1984): 110–117.

_____. *Feminism in Eighteenth-Century England*. Urbana: University of Illinois Press, 1982.

Scholes, Percy A. *The Great Dr. Burney*. 2 vols. New York: Oxford University Press, 1948.

Scott, Walter S. *The Bluestocking Ladies*. London: John Green, 1947.

Seeley, Leonard Benton. *Fanny Burney and Her Friends*. London: Seeley, 1890.

_____. *Mrs. Thrale, Afterwards Mrs. Piozzi*. London: Seeley, 1891.

Sherbo, Arthur. *English Sentimental Drama*. East Lansing: Michigan State University Press, 1957.

Simons, Judy. *Fanny Burney*. Totowa: Barnes and Noble, 1987.

Straub, Kristina. *Divided Fictions: Fanny Burney and Feminine Strategy*. Lexington: University of Kentucky Press, 1987.

Tanselle, G. Thomas. "External Fact as an Editorial Problem." *Studies in Bibliography* 32 (1979): 1–47.

Thrale, Hester. *Autobiography, Letters, and Literary Remains of Mrs. Piozzi*. Ed. A. Hayward. London: Longman, Green, Longman and Robbs, 1861.

_____. *The Thrales of Streatham Park*. Ed. Mary Morley Hyde. Cambridge, Mass.: Harvard University Press, 1977.

_____. *Thraliana*. Ed. Katharine C. Balderston. Oxford: The Clarendon Press, 1951.